Cities
Without
Suburbs

Cities Without Suburbs

David Rusk

\\\\/ Published by The Woodrow Wilson Center Press
Distributed by The Johns Hopkins University Press

Woodrow Wilson Center Special Studies

The Woodrow Wilson Center Press
Editorial Offices
370 L'Enfant Promenade, S.W.
Suite 704
Washington, D.C. 20024-2518 U.S.A.
telephone 202-287-3000, ext. 218

Distributed by
The Johns Hopkins University Press
Hampden Station
Baltimore, Maryland 21211
Order department telephone 1-800-537-5487

Printed in the United States of America

⊗ Printed on acid-free paper.

9 8 7 6

Library of Congress Cataloging-in-Publication Data

Rusk, David.
    Cities without suburbs / David Rusk.
        p.   cm. — (Woodrow Wilson Center special studies)
    Includes bibliographical references and index.
    ISBN 0-943875-49-8 (cloth). — ISBN 0-943875-50-1 (paper)
        1. Urban policy—United States.   2. Metropolitan government—
United States.   3. Metropolitan areas—United States.   I. Title.
II. Series.
HT123.R84   1993
307.76′0973—dc20

93-18815
                                                                    CIP

To
Delcia,
my wife
and
partner

Contents

List of Boxes

Preface

This short book is written for public policy makers. Its intended audience is our new president and his administration, U.S. senators and representatives, state governors and legislators, city and county elected officials—and key staff everywhere who behind the scenes help make American government work. I also wrote the book for thoughtful and concerned citizens who are prepared to think in a different way about what has happened in and around their communities and who will spur their public officials to take decisive action.

This book is intended to be argumentative. I have been cautious in neither characterizations nor conclusions. It is not my purpose for each page to be unassailable. The cold, clear light of scholarly criticism may show that I am a little wrong about some details. I am prepared for that. In terms of the big picture, I believe that I am right.

What I want to achieve is to help key policy makers and opinion leaders face the fact that racial and economic segregation is the heart of America's "urban problem." What has most surprised me upon returning to Washington, D.C., after twenty years in New Mexico, is that this fundamental issue is not even discussed!

First and foremost, this book is the product of my practical experience—political and managerial—as mayor of Albuquerque from 1977 to 1981. Four years as chief executive of the largest city in New Mexico may, in some readers' opinion, not qualify me to be an expert on what has been happening to America's cities. But Albuquerque is a bigger city—and its city hall runs a bigger city government—than "big league" cities such as Atlanta, Buffalo, Cincinnati, Minneapolis (and St. Paul), Oakland, Pittsburgh, and St. Louis. Within ten or twenty years at most, Albuquerque's population will surpass that of the cities of Boston, Cleveland, Denver, Kansas City, New Orleans, Seattle, and Washington, D.C.

All this because, as a "central city," Albuquerque is growing, and the others are shrinking! The reason why an Albuquerque grows and an Atlanta, Cleveland, or St. Louis shrinks—what I call a city's "elasticity"—lies at the heart of America's urban problem.

Other practical career experiences shape this book. Before becoming mayor, I spent three years as a state legislator in New Mexico and five years as a civil rights and antipoverty worker with the Washington Urban League. Also valuable was my federal government experience as the U.S. Manpower Administration's legislative services chief.

In addition, this book is the product of painstaking, hands-on research. I have passed endless days unearthing data from old census publications. My long backward look over the past four decades forced me laboriously to hand copy and then enter thousands of pieces of information into the data base of my personal computer. This past year I devoted all my time to researching what has been happening to America's 522 central cities in 320 metropolitan areas.

Well aware of the sad realities of urban America, I decided to write this book as an act of hope and faith. I believe that the problem this book addresses—the "urban problem"—is the toughest issue in American society. It goes right to the heart of the deep-rooted fears about race and social class that have had so much to do with shaping urban America today.

I have shared with others my strategies for reunifying city and suburbs, creating, in effect, "cities without suburbs." Many thoughtful people have responded "You're right, but what you propose is politically impossible! Be realistic!"

No one who has run for public office four times (twice successfully) or organized presidential campaigns locally can be insensitive to the daunting political difficulties my proposals face. But I am also a child of the civil rights movement. As Abraham Lincoln testified in his first inaugural address, miracles can be wrought in the American soul and spirit "when again touched, as surely they will be, by the angels of our better nature."

In his next-to-last 1992 campaign speech (at a postmidnight rally, coincidentally, at Albuquerque International Airport), then-Governor Bill Clinton said, "It's taken our country a long time to get into this mess. We're not going to solve it overnight.

But we can't even start solving it unless we have the courage to look our problems in the face.'' The president-to-be was talking about the economy. He could have been talking about America's urban problem. The goal of this book is to help us look the urban problem full in the face.

David Rusk

Washington, D.C.
March 1993

Acknowledgments

For many years I have conceived of this book, but it probably would not have been born without the assistance of Director Charles Blitzer and the Woodrow Wilson International Center for Scholars. For the summer of 1992, the Woodrow Wilson Center invited me to be a Guest Scholar on urban affairs. I am indebted to the Center for its gracious support and for the opportunity to exchange ideas with many stimulating colleagues. In particular, I appreciate the critical guidance from our "urban cluster"—Joe Tulchin, Blair Ruble, and Mary Bullock (all three staff members of the Center); Ed Bergman (University of North Carolina); John Walton (University of California at Davis); and my comrade-in-arms, Hank Savitch (University of Louisville).

I also received invaluable assistance from Daniel Green, my research associate this summer; from Joanne Graham and Lisa Kosow of the U.S. Census Bureau Library; and from the Business and Economics Division of the Martin Luther King Library in the District of Columbia.

Over the past year my work has been encouraged and supported by several organizations to which I am grateful, including the National Urban League, the Democratic Leadership Council, The Urban Institute, the Committee for Economic Development, Sterling Tucker Associates, the Progressive Policy Institute, the National League of Cities, and the Carnegie Corporation of New York.

In addition to the friends and colleagues who read and critiqued my work this year, I am particularly grateful to Dick Rowson, Joseph Brinley, and Carolee Belkin Walker at the Woodrow Wilson Center Press as well as to Barbara de Boinville for patient and professional editing.

Despite my debt to all who have helped me, the responsibility for the book's analysis and recommendations is purely mine.

Finally, I wish to thank my family—my mother, father, and brother, Rich, who are already veterans of one book collaboration; Gregory, who sacrificed his Macintosh; Patrick, our computer maven, who set up the initial spreadsheets and provided long-distance technical assistance; Monica and son-in-law, Mark, who constantly encouraged me; and my wife, Delcia, who, having shared my life's experience, has been my most valuable editor and contributor. Their love and support have sustained me.

Introduction: Framing the Issue

To discuss "urban policy" it is helpful to have a common view of the "urban problem." Economists debate urban labor supply, capital availability, and internal and external market opportunities. Housing experts discuss how to ensure adequate, affordable shelter, and transportation planners, how to move people and goods within and beyond urban areas. Public works administrators worry about water and sewer systems, storm drains, and power grids; environmentalists worry about urban air and water quality. Finally, local elected officials argue among themselves (and with their constituents) about how to pay for public wants. Each group sees its area of responsibility as part of the urban problem.

Jobs, housing, streets and highways, water and sewer systems, pollution, and revenues are common issues for urban areas everywhere, but collectively they do not seem to add up to America's urban problem. In fact, compared with most urban populations throughout the world, America does not really have an urban problem as such. Most urban Americans are better employed, better housed, better served by transportation systems and public facilities, and live in better environmental conditions than the rest of the world. America's real urban problem is the racial and economic segregation that has created an underclass in many of America's major urban areas.

Segregating poor urban Blacks and Hispanics has spawned physically decaying, revenue-strapped, poverty-impacted, crime-ridden "inner cities." These inner cities are isolated from their "outer cities"—wealthier, growing, largely White suburbs.

Debate over urban policy has focused on only a handful of America's largest inner cities. By contrast, this book will look at all urban areas and examine in detail more than 100 urban areas with populations of 200,000 or more. Also, by contrast, my focus will be on entire metropolitan areas—cities and suburbs.

This broader perspective will yield, I hope, greater clarity

1

about what has been happening in urban America. There are lessons to be learned from many urban areas that are rarely analyzed. There are bad lessons to be drawn from areas such as Harrisburg, Pennsylvania, and Syracuse, New York. There are success stories to be learned, for example, from Madison, Wisconsin, and my own Albuquerque.

In highly segregated urban areas—no matter how wealthy areawide—concentrated poverty, welfare dependency, and crime compound each other, and inner cities are failing. In more integrated urban areas—even when poorer areawide—poverty, dependency, and crime lack critical mass, and the cities are succeeding.

In about half of the country's large urban areas, social and economic inequities are severe. In the other half, however, good timing, good luck, and good public policy—which come to focus in what I call a city's "elasticity"—have combined to create more successful communities for Whites, Blacks, and Hispanics alike. In short, half of America's large urban areas needs to take some pointers from the other half about what works. Conversely, the other half needs to learn to avoid the path of failure shown by the first.

In the first chapter, I derive twenty-four "lessons" and four "laws" from what has been happening in urban America since World War II. The statistical analysis typically begins with the 1950 census and ends with the 1990 census. The first four lessons stated in Chapter I are supported by data drawn from the 320 metropolitan areas in the United States. Thereafter, to give the reader a more tangible feel for my observations, I illustrate the remaining general lessons by contrasting seven pairs of specific metropolitan areas: Houston and Detroit, Columbus and Cleveland, Nashville and Louisville, Indianapolis and Milwaukee, Albuquerque and Syracuse, Madison and Harrisburg, Raleigh and Richmond.

In Chapter II, "Characteristics of Metropolitan Areas," I take the lessons stated and illustrated in Chapter I and divide most of the large urban areas into five broad categories. For each of these broad categories, I then restate the key data used for Chapter I.

In Chapter III, I discuss strategies for "stretching" cities. These strategies are framed for action at the local, state, and federal levels. There is not a single strategy that, in conventional political terms, would be easy to accomplish. Our society has spent decades building up this mess. There will be no easy solutions. I believe that adopting these strategies—creating "cities without suburbs"—can profoundly transform the long-term outlook for failing central cities and help re-energize American society.

Chapter IV presents my conclusions and specific recommendations. Ultimately, reform of our cities must arise from broad-based citizen movements for change. Building popular movements is more art than science. Success lies more in the doing than in the telling.

Finally, I revisit some key ideas and acknowledge some additional considerations in an Afterword.

A clarifying comment on terminology. I often told Albuquerque audiences that New Mexico is one of the few places where a Puccini, a Pulaski, and a Goldstein could all be called "Anglo." Throughout the book, when I refer to "White," I mean "Anglo"—that is, non-Hispanic whites. And, contrary to commonly accepted editorial style, I will refer to Whites, Blacks, and Hispanics with coequal capital letters. I do not mean to slight either the problems or achievements of urban Asian and Native Americans by not focusing on them. From my analysis, however, it is only around Whites, Blacks, and Hispanics that social and political attitudes in America revolve with sufficient force and magnitude to shape patterns of urban growth.

Chapter I

Lessons from Urban America

Despite the romance of the frontier, the true land of opportunity in America for over 150 years has been the cities. From farms and foreign lands, urban immigrants flocked into the cities, seeking better schools, better jobs, better health care—in short, a better life. What lessons can be drawn from a broad look at what has been happening in urban America over the last forty years?

Lesson 1: The real city is the total metropolitan area—city and suburb.

At the end of World War II, urban America was still the inner cities. There were hardly any outer cities. The suburban movement was just starting. The country's biggest cities were booming and bursting at the seams. Drawn by the war industries, millions had left farms and small towns to pack into the cities.

In 1950 almost 70 percent of the population of 168 metropolitan areas lived in 193 central cities. (For an explanation of Census Bureau terms, see Box 1.1.) City residents attended the same city school system. They used the city parks and libraries. They rode city buses, streetcars, and subways to blue- and white-collar jobs within the city or, occasionally, to nearby factories. They fought for control of the same city hall. Although there were often fierce rivalries among ethnic and racial groups, common public institutions were unifying forces (except in the segregated South).

Today the situation is reversed. By 1990 over 60 percent of the population of 320 metropolitan areas lived in suburbs. Equally as important, suburbs no longer simply served as bedroom communities for workers with city-based jobs. By 1990 a majority of jobs in metro areas were located in suburbs.

5

Box 1.1 What Is a Metropolitan Area?

According to the U.S. Census Bureau, a "metropolitan area" (Metropolitan Statistical Area, MSA, or metro area) is "a geographic area consisting of a large population nucleus together with adjacent communities which have a high degree of economic and social integration with that nucleus." In short, a metro area is a city and its suburbs.

Each metro area must include a "central city" that, with contiguous, densely settled territory, constitutes a Census Bureau–defined urbanized area of at least 50,000 people. If the largest city has fewer than 50,000 people, the area must have a total population of at least 100,000.

In 1910 the Census Bureau first introduced "metropolitan districts." Since then it has used many different methodologies to define metro areas, but by 1950 it had settled on using entire counties as the building blocks of metro areas. Counties outside of the "central county" in which the "central city" is located are added based on commuting patterns of workers into the central city or central county.

In recent decades the Census Bureau has recognized additional central cities beyond the historic focal points of many metro areas. Now there are 522 central cities in 320 metro areas. A metro area's title may include up to three central cities, such as "Tampa–St. Petersburg–Clearwater FL MSA."

Seventeen of the largest urban regions are designated as Consolidated Metropolitan Statistical Areas (CMSAs) composed of two or more Primary Metropolitan Statistical Areas (PMSAs). In New England (where counties are not primary local governments), the Census Bureau for statistical purposes has designated New England County Metropolitan Areas (NECMAs).

In this book the basic unit of analysis will be a MSA, PMSA, or NECMA. In metro areas of more than one central city, only the first named city will be treated as the central city (for example, Tampa for Tampa–St. Petersburg–Clearwater, Florida).

All metro areas will be analyzed as they were defined as of June 30, 1989. A metro area's population in 1950 will include the populations in 1950 of all counties considered part of the metro area in 1990 rather than how the metro area was conceived under 1950 conditions.

The traditional city no longer is "the place to be" to find a better life. In fact, the housing, jobs, schools, and services are worse in many inner cities than they are in the neighboring suburbs. Any attack on urban social and economic problems must treat suburb and city as indivisible parts of a whole.

Lesson 2: Most of America's Blacks, Hispanics, and Asians live in urban areas.

Forty years ago the country's 15 million Blacks were still substantially rural and southern, although a tremendous migration into cities north and south had been under way since the Great Depression. Similarly, most of the country's Hispanics were scattered in rural areas and small cities located largely throughout the Southwest. Asian-Americans, always an urban people, were heavily concentrated in West Coast cities.

In 1950 America's population was about 86 to 87 percent White and 13 to 14 percent minority (including Native Americans).[1] Forty years later America is 27 percent minority, and over 80 percent of all minorities live in metropolitan areas. In fact, the majority of all Blacks, Hispanics, and Asians live in just thirty metropolitan areas.[2]

Today minorities as well as opportunity are concentrated in urban areas. Social and economic equality is a goal that can be achieved only by what happens in urban areas.

Lesson 3: Since World War II, all urban growth has been low-density, suburban style.

The 1950 census was the high watermark for most of America's big cities. Of the twelve largest cities, ten (all except New York and Los Angeles) hit their population peaks in the 1950 census.

Thereafter, Washington, Wall Street, Detroit, Hollywood, and Madison Avenue made middle-class families an offer they could not refuse: the American Dream. Sustained economic growth, cheap home mortgages, affordable private cars, and federally subsidized highways—all touted on big screens and small—made that dream house with its own yard, quiet neighborhood, local school, and nearby shopping possible for millions of families. Compared with staying put in many city neighborhoods, suburbia was a bargain. Urban America became Suburban America.

Everyone knows this. What is not always recognized is how universal this pattern has been in postwar America.

A key measure is "population density." Population density measures how many people live per square mile. What has happened to population densities in America depends on the frame of reference.

Time-traveling from the 1790s, Daniel Boone would find the whole country intolerably densely populated in the 1990s with its 245 million people.[3] Long-time residents of rural areas and small towns may well feel that the countryside is getting "too crowded" today with new suburban subdivisions springing up around them.

But within America's 522 central cities, population density has declined by 50 percent![4] From 5,873 persons per square mile in 1950, overall density dropped to 2,937 persons per square mile in 1990. And that happened almost everywhere—in big cities and small. In 1950, for example, there were thirty-eight cities with densities of 10,000 or more persons per square mile. Over the next forty years all thirty-eight lost density. By 1990 there were only fifteen cities with densities of 10,000 or more persons per square mile.

During this period 107 of 522 central cities actually increased their population densities, but almost all of these were well below the average national density in 1950. In effect, most were thinly populated areas waiting to become more populated, but still low-density, "cities."

Only five cities with above-average densities in 1950 and a half dozen others that had densities just below average actually increased their densities. All were targets of Hispanic immigration.

Miami, Miami Beach, and Hialeah, Florida, were all centers of Cuban and Central American immigration in which the Hispanic population comprised 62 percent, 47 percent, and 88 percent, respectively, by 1990.

The Pacific Rim's Ellis Island was the greater Los Angeles area, as Hispanic and Asian immigrants filled Los Angeles, Long Beach, Burbank, Pasadena, Pomona, and, in neighboring Orange County, Anaheim and Santa Ana. In fact, one-third of

Los Angeles County's population in 1990 was foreign-born—half having arrived in the past decade!

Other immigration focused on the greater New York area, the traditional port of entry. Immigrants cushioned New York City against greater population loss (only −7 percent between 1950 and 1990). Immigrants also kept smaller cities like Paterson, Elizabeth, and Perth Amboy, New Jersey, filled up to higher than usual densities.

In short, the only cities in America that swam against the suburban stream were cities swimming with the immigrant stream. A certain natural clustering of new immigrants, large families (including extended families), low incomes, and a degree of anti-Hispanic or anti-Asian discrimination in neighboring communities combined to sustain growing densities in these port-of-entry cities. Everywhere else, most middle-class, White Americans for the past forty years have chosen to raise young families in low-density communities rather than high-density cities.

Lesson 4: For a city's population to grow, the city must be "elastic."

Think of a city as a map drawn on a rubber sheet. If there is a great deal of vacant land within existing city limits, that city's population density is low. The city has room for new population growth by filling in undeveloped land. In effect, the rubber sheet map is slack. Facing growth opportunities, the city is still elastic within its boundaries because of its low population density. It can stretch upward to accommodate new growth.[5]

On the other hand, what if the city is already densely populated? There is little or no vacant land to develop. Its rubber sheet map is stretched taut within its existing boundaries.

That high-density city cannot become more dense. (That is not a lifestyle that most postwar, middle-class families "buy.") The high-density city's only path to growth is to expand its boundaries. It must stretch the edges of its rubber sheet map to take in new territory. It must become more elastic outward rather than upward.

The most common method by which a city acquires new territory is annexation. Typically, a city annexes undeveloped land. More rarely, an annexation brings in an existing community.

Stretching the edges of the municipal map often creates ten-
sion—outside resistance from those to be annexed and inside
resistance from a city's current residents. Annexation is not always easy.

How much did cities utilize each mechanism—filling in vacant
land and annexing additional territory? Only about 20 percent of
all cities actually increased their densities. For many other cities,
however, in-fill development was combined with boundary expansion (which often tended to mask the degree of in-fill
development).

Boundary expansion contributed most to municipal elasticity.
Between 1950 and 1990 more than four-fifths of the 522 central
cities expanded their boundaries by 10 percent or more. The
municipal expansion champion was Anchorage, Alaska. By ab-
sorbing its entire surrounding borough the city of Anchorage
grew from 12.5 square miles to 1,697.7 square miles (13,482 percent)! Overall, the 522 central cities expanded from 10,513
square miles to 27,728 square miles (164 percent, or 149 percent
if Anchorage's massive land grab is discounted).

On the threshold of the era of the suburban lifestyle, the cities
with the greatest elasticity had vacant city land to develop *and*
the political and legal tools to annex new land. These I will call
"elastic cities." At the other end of the spectrum were the "inelastic cities"—typically older cities already built out at higher
than average densities and, for a variety of reasons, unable or
unwilling to expand their city limits.

This pattern of urban development is sufficiently universal (at
least, in America) to embolden me to state the first law of urban
dynamics: *only elastic cities grow*.

This concept of a city's elasticity is the central idea of this
book. Why have some cities been elastic and others have not?
What are the demographic, economic, and social consequences
of inelasticity? If being an elastic city is essential to economic,
social, and fiscal health, what can be done to make inelastic
cities elastic again or, at least, to benefit as if they were elastic?

Summary data for all metro areas support the first few lessons I
have presented. The succeeding lessons are best illustrated by
contrasting specific metro areas that I have paired: Detroit-
Houston, Columbus-Cleveland, Nashville-Louisville, Indi-
anapolis-Milwaukee, Albuquerque-Syracuse, Madison-Harris-

burg, and Raleigh-Richmond. At first glance several of the metro areas paired may seem to have nothing in common. All pairs, however, have been matched in terms of two key characteristics. First, from 1950 to 1990 the metro areas in each pair added roughly equal numbers of new residents as measured by net growth of the metro population and by new-home buyers (Table 1.1). (How "new-home buyers" is derived is discussed on pages 14–15.) Second, by 1990 the metro areas of each pair had roughly the same percentage of Black population metro-wide (Table 1.2).

Although the metro areas in each pair are equivalent in new-home buyers and percentage of Black population, the relative elasticity of the principal central cities in each pair is not the same. The more elastic city or area is listed first; the less elastic city or area is listed second. (For example, Houston is more elastic than Detroit.)[6]

TABLE 1.1
EACH PAIR OF METRO AREAS HAS ABOUT THE
SAME NUMBER OF NEW-HOME BUYERS

Metro area	New-home buyers 1950–90
Houston, Tex.	2,400,986
Detroit, Mich.	1,957,962
Columbus, Ohio	648,617
Cleveland, Ohio	707,740
Nashville, Tenn.	483,118
Louisville, Ky.	417,691
Indianapolis, Ind.	522,700
Milwaukee, Wis.	427,242
Albuquerque, N. Mex.	334,904
Syracuse, N.Y.	251,473
Madison, Wis.	197,728
Harrisburg, Pa.	226,448
Raleigh, N.C.	431,615
Richmond, Va.	429,830

TABLE 1.2
EACH PAIR OF METRO AREAS HAS ABOUT THE SAME
PERCENTAGE OF BLACKS IN THE POPULATION

Metro area	Percentage of Blacks in the metro population
Houston, Tex.	19%
Detroit, Mich.	21
Columbus, Ohio	12
Cleveland, Ohio	19
Nashville, Tenn.	15
Louisville, Ky.	13
Indianapolis, Ind.	14
Milwaukee, Wis.	14
Albuquerque, N. Mex.	3
Syracuse, N.Y.	6
Madison, Wis.	3
Harrisburg, Pa.	7
Raleigh, N.C.	25
Richmond, Va.	29

Lesson 5: Almost all metro areas have grown.

It is easy to label Detroit, Cleveland, and Milwaukee "dying Frostbelt areas" and Houston, Raleigh, and Albuquerque "booming Sunbelt areas." The truth is, however, that the populations of all of these Frostbelt areas have grown as *total metropolitan areas*. In fact, the populations of most metropolitan areas have grown over the past four decades.[7]

Table 1.3 presents the metro population growth of the seven pairs of metro areas. Metro areas containing elastic cities have had higher growth rates than metro areas with inelastic cities. These metro areas began at lower population levels. However, in 1990 the metro areas containing the inelastic cities were still somewhat more populous (with the exception of Nashville, which has edged ahead of Louisville). The inelastic areas began at much higher population levels and added to that base.

Growth rates, of course, are a function of how much is added to how large an initial base. Each additional resident contributes

TABLE 1.3
ALMOST ALL METRO AREAS HAVE GROWN

Metro area	Metro population			Percentage change 1950–90
	1950	1990	Change 1950–90	
Houston, Tex.	900,951	3,301,937	2,400,986	174%
Detroit, Mich.	3,245,981	4,382,299	1,136,318	35
Columbus, Ohio	728,802	1,377,419	648,617	89
Cleveland, Ohio	1,532,574	1,831,122	298,548	19
Nashville, Tenn.	501,908	985,026	483,118	96
Louisville, Ky.	635,037	952,662	317,625	50
Indianapolis, Ind.	727,122	1,249,822	522,700	72
Milwaukee, Wis.	1,014,211	1,432,149	417,938	41
Albuquerque, N. Mex.	145,673	480,577	334,904	230
Syracuse, N.Y.	465,114	659,864	194,750	42
Madison, Wis.	169,357	367,085	197,728	117
Harrisburg, Pa.	398,706	587,986	189,280	47
Raleigh, N.C.	303,865	735,480	431,615	142
Richmond, Va.	463,064	865,640	402,576	87

to a higher rate of growth where there is a smaller initial population base than a larger initial population base. Thus, the rates of population growth among elastic areas (72 percent to 230 percent) were much higher than growth rates among inelastic areas (19 percent to 87 percent).

Do great disparities in *rates* of population growth make a difference? Of course they do. For an area to double its population (Columbus, Nashville, Madison) or triple its population (Houston, Albuquerque) creates a different business climate, a different community climate, even a "boom town" psychology, than exist in an area that grows more slowly.

However, the spectacular rates of population growth of some metro areas have obscured the fact that less spectacularly expanding areas have added hundreds of thousands or millions of new residents. For example, from 1950 to 1990 the Houston metro area added 2.4 million people (net), but the Detroit metro area added 1.1 million people (net) as well. In addition, Houston's and Detroit's growth were much closer in terms of numbers of families looking for new homes—the key to how local jurisdictions grow within the same metro area.

Lesson 6: Some central cities have grown; others have shrunk.

Central to the urban problem is *how* different metro areas have grown. As Table 1.4 shows, the inelastic cities suffered catastrophic population losses. Metro population growth occurred entirely in suburbs outside these cities' boundaries. In sharp contrast, the elastic cities grew substantially.

Table 1.1 earlier summarized the effect of these sharply contrasting growth patterns (1950–90) in terms of new-home buyers. How is this concept of "new-home buyers" derived?

Since household sizes have fallen throughout America (except in cities with recent immigration), any additional population must be accommodated in new housing, typically in new subdi-

TABLE 1.4
SOME CENTRAL CITIES HAVE GROWN;
OTHERS HAVE SHRUNK

| Metro area | City population | | | Percentage change 1950–90 |
	1950	1990	Change 1950–90	
Houston, Tex.	596,163	1,630,553	1,034,390	174%
Detroit, Mich.	1,849,568	1,027,924	−821,644	−44
Columbus, Ohio	375,901	632,910	257,009	68
Cleveland, Ohio	914,808	505,616	−409,192	−45
Nashville, Tenn.	174,307	488,374	314,067	180
Louisville, Ky.	369,129	269,063	−100,066	−27
Indianapolis, Ind.	427,173	731,327	304,154	71
Milwaukee, Wis.	637,392	628,088	−9,304	−1
Albuquerque, N. Mex.	96,815	384,736	287,921	297
Syracuse, N.Y.	220,583	163,860	−56,723	−26
Madison, Wis.	96,056	191,282	95,226	99
Harrisburg, Pa.	89,544	52,376	−37,168	−42
Raleigh, N.C.	65,679	207,951	142,272	217
Richmond, Va.	230,310	203,056	−27,254	−12

visions. For an elastic area (Houston or Columbus, for example) "new-home buyers" is the same as net metro population growth. (The calculation of new-home buyers includes all household members.) For an inelastic area, however, new homes must be provided for newcomers to the metro area and for current residents moving from the city to the suburbs. For an inelastic area "new-home buyers" is net metro population growth and the central city's net loss of population. For an inelastic area "new-home buyers" is identical to suburban population growth. I have resisted, however, labeling it "suburban growth" because city and suburb potentially competed to house that population.

How well different cities succeeded in that competition is the heart of the issue. For example, the "booming" Houston area had to accommodate 2,400,986 million residents in new housing, while the "dying" Detroit area had to provide new housing for 1,957,962 (Table 1.1).

Lesson 7: Low-density cities can grow through in-fill; high-density cities cannot.

What was the situation of our sample cities in 1950 as the American Dream picked up momentum? The average density for all 522 central cities in 1950 was 5,873 persons per square mile. Albuquerque and Houston were well below the national average (Table 1.5). They would have accommodated some additional growth within existing city limits. Nashville might have had a little "room at the inn" as well. But even Raleigh, Richmond, and Madison appear by 1950 to have surpassed the density standards associated with the emerging American Dream.

No city after 1950 expanded beyond 5,000 persons per square mile except for cities with Hispanic immigration mentioned above; New Britain and New London, Connecticut (small coastal cities that just edged past the 5,000 per square mile mark); and seven booming college towns—Annapolis, Maryland (U.S. Naval Academy), Davis (University of California), East Lansing (Michigan State), Evanston, Illinois (Northwestern University), New Brunswick, New Jersey (Rutgers University), State College (Penn State), and West Lafayette, Indiana (Purdue). If city planners in 1950 had had crystal balls, they would have seen that any city with a density of 5,000 or more persons

TABLE 1.5
LOW-DENSITY CITIES CAN GROW THROUGH IN-FILL;
HIGH-DENSITY CITIES CANNOT

Metro area	City density (persons per square mile) 1950	City density as a percentage of national average density, 1950
Houston, Tex.	3,726	63%
Detroit, Mich.	13,249	226
Columbus, Ohio	9,541	162
Cleveland, Ohio	12,197	208
Nashville, Tenn.	4,333	74
Louisville, Ky.	9,251	158
Indianapolis, Ind.	7,739	132
Milwaukee, Wis.	12,748	217
Albuquerque, N. Mex.	2,021	34
Syracuse, N.Y.	8,719	148
Madison, Wis.	6,237	106
Harrisburg, Pa.	14,213	208
Raleigh, N.C.	5,971	102
Richmond, Va.	6,208	106

per square mile would have to look for new land, new immigrants, or new college students to add to its population.

Lesson 8: Elastic cities expand their city limits; inelastic cities do not.

Elastic cities did not just fill up vacant areas within existing city
limits. They expanded their city limits aggressively (Table 1.6).
Houston, Columbus, Albuquerque, Madison, and Raleigh grew
through aggressive annexation of surrounding areas. After the
earlier pace of annexation had slowed, the city of Nashville and
the city of Indianapolis expanded dramatically through consolidation with their home counties to create new, unified
governments.

By contrast, almost without exception, inelastic cities entered
the postwar growth era locked within their existing boundaries.

TABLE 1.6
ELASTIC CITIES EXPAND THEIR CITY LIMITS;
INELASTIC CITIES DO NOT

Metro area	City area (square miles)		Percentage change 1950–1990
	1950	1990	
Houston, Tex.	160	540	237%
Detroit, Mich.	139	139	0
Columbus, Ohio	39	191	385
Cleveland, Ohio	75	77	3
Nashville, Tenn.	22	473	2,051
Louisville, Ky.	40	62	56
Indianapolis, Ind.	55	362	555
Milwaukee, Wis.	50	96	92
Albuquerque, N. Mex.	48	132	176
Syracuse, N.Y.	25	25	0
Madison, Wis.	15	58	275
Harrisburg, Pa.	6	8	29
Raleigh, N.C.	11	88	550
Richmond, Va.	37	60	62

The city limits of Detroit and Syracuse did not budge. The city of Cleveland added only two square miles, as did the city of Harrisburg. (Harrisburg's proportional growth, adding roughly one-third to its 6.3 square miles, might look significant, but the effect was minuscule within a 1,991–square mile metro area.)

Lesson 9: When a city stops growing, it starts shrinking.

In the early postwar period, Milwaukee, Louisville, and Richmond continued to expand in population and in area (by forty-six, twenty-two, and twenty-three square miles, respectively). Between 1950 and 1960 Milwaukee almost doubled its area and added over 100,000 new residents (about 16 percent growth). Then, as annexation stopped, Milwaukee peaked out. Since its 1960 peak Milwaukee has lost all of that added population. In 1990 its population was slightly below its 1950 level.

Box 1.2 New York City, 1790–1990

My analysis has focused on different cities' "elasticity" amid metro growth over the past forty years, but *all* cities were elastic in their youth. New York City serves as a historical microcosm for urban development patterns everywhere.

In 1790 the city of New York, located on the tip of Manhattan Island, was the country's largest city, surpassing Philadelphia, Boston, and Baltimore. It had 33,131 residents. Barely 16,000 people were scattered in villages and farms in the surrounding boroughs (about fifty people per square mile).

By 1890 the city of New York had packed 1.4 million residents onto Manhattan Island. Linked to the city of New York by the Brooklyn Bridge, the city of Brooklyn was the Phoenix of the nineteenth century, increasing its population twentyfold between 1840 and 1890. The other boroughs, however, were still relatively lightly populated.[1]

In 1898 New York's state legislature created a new New York City by combining the five boroughs and abolishing all other municipal governments, such as the city of Brooklyn. This legislative act, approved over fierce lobbying opposition from wealthy suburbanites in Brooklyn, created the world's largest city (3.4 million in 1900) and the country's first metropolitan government.

Packed with new European immigrants, the old city of New York (Manhattan) had been approaching its capacity. It would still grow another 23 percent in population, but would peak out by 1910. Consolidation made the city of New York elastic again, above all through acquiring more than 200 square miles of lightly settled land in the Bronx, Queens, and Staten Island.

For the next fifty years much of New York City's "suburban" growth occurred within its own city limits. Brooklyn grew another 135 percent, peaking at 2.3 million in 1950. The Bronx grew 625 percent (to 1.5 million) before flattening out in 1950. Queens grew 1,200 percent, finally peaking in 1970 at 2.0 million. Now approaching 400,000 residents, Staten Island's growth has not yet stopped. These earlier "suburbs" may have been subway-

---

In similar fashion Louisville and Richmond continued to grow in population while geographic expansion was under way. Louisville added 6 percent until 1960; Richmond, about 8 percent until 1970. Then, when geographic expansion halted, their populations began dropping. The drop in Louisville was precip-

and-trolley suburbs rather than the auto-based suburbs of the postwar decades, but they were suburbs all the same.

When the Census Bureau in 1910 conceived of metropolitan districts, it designated New York City as the hub of northern New Jersey (Newark and Jersey City) and Westchester County. New York City constituted over 80 percent of the population of this region. Since then the definition of greater New York has expanded slowly. By 1950 New York City was still 61 percent of the region's population.

Thereafter, the suburban movement blossomed beyond New York's city limits. Nassau and Suffolk counties exploded to 2.6 million people by 1970. Fairfield County, Connecticut, doubled to 828,000 by 1990, drawing off many of Manhattan's richest executives and corporate headquarters. Commuting patterns extended the greater New York area far down into middle New Jersey. The counties there doubled and tripled in population.

For five decades, while New York City *was* largely its own suburbs, it was one of the most successful urban communities. New York City's schools, hospitals, and city services were among the nation's best. With all of its warts, New York City was a great magnet for those seeking a better life—and it largely delivered!

But 1950 was the watershed. From 1900 to 1950, New York City captured over 50 percent of its suburban growth; after 1950 it contributed −13 percent to its suburban growth. By 1990 New York City only accounted for 41 percent of regional population.

When it was truly a metro government, New York City was enormously successful. When it slipped into being the central city of a metropolitan region expanding far beyond its borders, its fabled problems began. New York City needs another ''Generation of 1898.''

1. In 1890 the population densities of New York City's future boroughs were Manhattan, 64,629 people per square mile; Brooklyn, 11,019; the Bronx, 2,049; Queens, 770; and Staten Island, 857. Their 1890 population densities would have ranked the latter three boroughs in the lowest 10 percent of all ''suburbanizing'' communities sixty years later.

itous (−31 percent, from its 1960 peak), while Richmond's population erosion has been more gradual (−19 percent, from its 1970 peak). Richmond's population is now below its 1950 level, while Louisville has turned its population clock back to the 1920s!

Lesson 10: Elastic cities "capture" suburban growth; inelastic cities "contribute" to suburban growth.

As I have shown, all postwar growth has been in the suburban mode—low-density development emphasizing detached, single-family homes. Elastic cities had large inventories of undeveloped land or were able to annex undeveloped land. They captured much of this suburban-style growth within their own municipal boundaries.

Inelastic cities could not grow either through in-fill or annexation. They could not compete with new suburbs in offering the desired suburban-style model for family life. Incapable of capturing a share of suburban-type development, inelastic cities actually contributed White, middle-class families to the new suburbs. In recent years in areas such as Washington, D.C., and Atlanta, a rapidly growing Black middle class has moved to the suburbs as well.

Table 1.7 sums up the effect in terms of a city's "capture or contribute" percentage. The "capture or contribute" percentage is calculated by dividing a city's net population growth by the new-home buyers. In effect, I am calculating the score in a city's competition with its suburbs for middle-class families.

Houston captured 43 percent of its new-home buyers, while Detroit contributed −42 percent to the suburbs' new-home buyers. Columbus captured 40 percent, Cleveland contributed −58 percent, and so forth down the list. (Milwaukee and Richmond have broken about even to this point, but are playing out losing hands unless they can radically change their cards.)

These metro areas illustrate our first law of urban dynamics: only elastic cities grow. But the first law begs a key question. Why did some cities stop expanding their city limits while other cities continued to grow?

Lesson 11: Bad state laws can hobble cities.

State laws differ concerning the power they give municipalities to expand. In New England, for example, the political map has long been set—in some cases since colonial times. New England state laws do not even provide for municipal annexation. In other regions state laws attach conditions that can severely limit a municipality's practical ability to annex additional territory.

TABLE 1.7
ELASTIC CITIES "CAPTURE" SUBURBAN GROWTH;
INELASTIC CITIES "CONTRIBUTE" TO SUBURBAN GROWTH

Metro area	City population change 1950–90	Metro new-home buyers 1950–1990	City capture/ contribute percentage
Houston, Tex.	1,034,390	2,400,986	43%
Detroit, Mich.	−821,644	1,957,962	−42
Columbus, Ohio	257,009	648,617	40
Cleveland, Ohio	−409,192	707,740	−58
Nashville, Tenn.	314,067	483,118	65
Louisville, Ky.	−100,066	417,691	−24
Indianapolis, Ind.	304,154	522,700	58
Milwaukee, Wis.	−9,304	427,242	−2
Albuquerque, N. Mex.	287,921	334,904	86
Syracuse, N.Y.	−56,723	251,473	−23
Madison, Wis.	95,206	197,728	48
Harrisburg, Pa.	−37,168	226,448	−16
Raleigh, N.C.	142,272	431,615	33
Richmond, Va.	−27,254	429,830	−6

Annexation may be allowed only upon voluntary petition by property owners. Sometimes an affirmative vote of affected land owners is required (or even approval by voters in the annexing municipality). Such restrictions on annexation authority are found most often in the Northeast and Midwest.

Table 1.8 summarizes the different cities' annexation powers and constraints under state law. In Houston, Detroit, Syracuse, Milwaukee, and Madison, annexation can be initiated only by affected property owners—a severe practical limitation on a municipality's legal ability to initiate expansion. Yet Houston and Madison have annexed vigorously, while Detroit and Syracuse have been stagnant. (Milwaukee almost doubled its area in the 1950s and 1960s and then stopped.)

Columbus and Cleveland have worked within identical ground rules, including the difficult (and uncommon) hurdle of securing county government acquiescence. Yet Columbus has been an aggressive annexer, while Cleveland has expanded hardly at all.

TABLE 1.8
BAD STATE LAWS CAN HOBBLE CITIES

Metro area	Municipal annexation			Approval by voters		Approval by county government
	Authorized by state law	Begun by property owner petition	Begun by city council action	Within annexed area	Within annexing city	
Houston, Tex.	Yes	Yes	[No]	[Yes]	No	No
Detroit, Mich.	Yes	Yes	[No]	[Yes]	[Yes]	No
Columbus, Ohio	Yes	Yes	Yes	[Yes]	No	[Yes]
Cleveland, Ohio	Yes	Yes	Yes	[Yes]	No	[Yes]
Nashville, Tenn.	Yes	Yes	Yes	[Yes]	[Yes]	No
Louisville, Ky.	Yes	No	Yes	No	No	No
Indianapolis, Ind.	Yes	Yes	Yes	No	No	No
Milwaukee, Wis.	Yes	Yes	[No]	[Yes]	No	No
Albuquerque, N. Mex.	Yes	Yes	Yes	[Yes]	No	No
Syracuse, N.Y.	Yes	Yes	[No]	[Yes]	No	No
Madison, Wis.	Yes	Yes	[No]	[Yes]	No	No
Harrisburg, Pa.	Yes	Yes	Yes	No	No	No
Raleigh, N.C.	Yes	Yes	Yes	No	No	No
Richmond, Va.	Yes	Yes	Yes	No	No	[Yes]

NOTE: Adverse requirements are highlighted by brackets.

Louisville and Harrisburg are favored with the most pro-annexation legal authority. Both cities can initiate and complete annexations by city council action without any further approvals (including the consent of those to be annexed). Both, however, have expanded minimally.

Differences in the annexation ground rules clearly do not explain the dramatic differences in boundary expansion among these sample cities.

Lesson 12: Neighbors can trap cities.

In some states a municipality cannot expand beyond its home county. By 1950 a few inelastic cities in America had largely filled up small home counties. Other inelastic cities had been transformed into their own counties or into "independent cities" with boundaries that could not expand.[8] By contrast, most elastic cities are located in counties that are geographically much larger; small central cities have room to grow very large.

In all states, however, one municipality cannot annex property within another municipality, regardless of the disparity in size. This can be the most insurmountable barrier to annexation.

A central city's expansion can be blocked by competing municipalities. Many older cities became gradually surrounded by smaller cities, towns, and villages. Newer central cities often faced only farmland, swamp, or sagebrush.

Table 1.9 shows the "elbowroom" each of the sample cities had in 1950. No city had come close to filling up its home county; municipal areas ranged from 1 percent to 23 percent of home-county areas. Cleveland, however, was completely hemmed in by Lake Erie on the north, and by twenty smaller municipalities ringing its city limits. Detroit was bounded by the Detroit River (an international boundary) and fifteen municipalities enclosing 75 percent of its city limits. Regardless of state laws, Cleveland and Detroit had nowhere to grow.

As evidenced by the growth in home-county populations outside the city limits, there was certainly room for population expansion within home counties in 1950 (even around Detroit and Cleveland).[9] Wayne County, for example, added 498,046 new residents outside of Detroit, while Cuyahoga County added 431,800 outside of Cleveland. Both Detroit and Cleveland, however, were blocked from capturing any of that growth. All growth occurred in suburban municipalities or in outlying unincorporated areas blocked off by the *cordon sanitaire* of suburban towns and villages.

Yet none of the other inelastic cities (Louisville, Milwaukee, Syracuse, Harrisburg, Richmond) was largely surrounded by existing municipalities. What other factors could have affected their ability to expand?

Lesson 13: Old cities are complacent; young cities are ambitious.

Certainly one clear distinction between elastic and inelastic cities is age: elastic cities are younger than inelastic cities. Table 1.10 lists the census at which each city first exceeded the 100,000 population milestone.

On the average the inelastic cities passed 100,000 or more residents around 1890, while the elastic cities did not reach that milestone until about 1930. The "average" of 1930, however,

TABLE 1.9
MOST CITIES HAD ROOM TO GROW BETWEEN 1950 AND 1990

| City | Home county | City area as a percentage of home county area | | Percentage of city limits enclosed by other municipalities 1950 | Balance of home county population growth 1950–90 | Percentage change in home county population 1950–90 |
		1950	1990			
Houston, Tex.	Harris	9%	31%	10%	976,824	464%
Detroit, Mich.	Wayne	23	23	75	498,046	85
Columbus, Ohio	Franklin	7	35	15	201,018	91
Cleveland, Ohio	Cuyahoga	17	17	100	431,800	87
Nashville, Tenn.	Davidson	4	94	1	–125,041	–85
Louisville, Ky.	Jefferson	10	16	30	280,338	243
Indianapolis, Ind.	Marion	14	91	25	–58,772	–47
Milwaukee, Wis.	Milwaukee	21	40	25	97,532	42
Albuquerque, N. Mex.	Bernalillo	4	11	0	46,983	96
Syracuse, N.Y.	Onondaga	3	3	10	183,977	152
Madison, Wis.	Dane	1	5	20	102,522	140
Harrisburg, Pa.	Dauphin	1	1	20	77,197	71
Raleigh, N.C.	Wake	1	11	0	144,658	204
Richmond, Va.	Ind. City	N/A	N/A	0	N/A	N/A

TABLE 1.10
Inelastic Cities Are Older than Elastic Cities

City	Census when the population exceeded 100,000
Houston, Tex.	1920
Detroit, Mich.	1880
Columbus, Ohio	1900
Cleveland, Ohio	1880
Nashville, Tenn.	1910
Louisville, Ky.	1870
Indianapolis, Ind.	1890
Milwaukee, Wis.	1880
Albuquerque, N. Mex.	1960
Syracuse, N.Y.	1900
Madison, Wis.	1970
Harrisburg, Pa.	1920[a]
Raleigh, N.C.	1970
Richmond, Va.	1910

[a]Census when the population exceeded 50,000.

masks an important difference: Houston, Columbus, Nashville, and Indianapolis passed the 100,000 population mark only a decade or two after the inelastic cities did; Albuquerque, Madison, and Raleigh are truly young cities.

What transformed the futures of Houston, Columbus, Nashville, and Indianapolis was, in large measure, the attitude of their community leadership (with citizen support). Houston and Columbus have been very expansionist through aggressive annexation (despite limitations on their legal powers). Even more striking, the leadership of Nashville and Indianapolis transformed their communities through successful city-county consolidations. Without city-county consolidation, which lifted both cities out of slow erosion, the current status of Nashville and Indianapolis would probably be little different from that of Louisville and Milwaukee.

In short, on the eve of the suburban era, older, established cities tended to be complacent. Already centers of national or regional wealth, they focused on dividing up the pie rather than on making the pie larger. By 1950 the shift of people, jobs, and

---

Box 1.3 Annexation and the Federal Voting Rights Act

Since 1971, a new hurdle has existed for many municipalities' annexation powers—the federal Voting Rights Act.

Under section 5, municipalities in all or sections of 29 states with large Black, Hispanic, or Native American populations have been required to clear proposed annexations with the United States Department of Justice.

The federal concern has been that by annexing predominantly White outlying areas, municipalities would dilute the growing political strength of Blacks and Hispanics.

According to Justice Department sources, over the past twenty-one years, the Justice Department has objected to 518 proposed annexations. To place this number in perspective, that is 1.5 percent of the 35,081 annexations submitted for review.[1]

Of these contested annexations, only 45—or 0.13 percent of the total—were ultimately prevented by either Justice Department objections or the federal courts. Many contested annexations were resolved by changes in the political system to enhance minority representation. Typically, such reforms involved shifting from at-large to districted local elections.

Perhaps the most famous and bitterly contested annexation was Richmond's annexation of 23 square miles of Chesterfield County in 1970. For seven years thereafter, federal courts blocked further city elections until the case was finally decided by the U.S. Supreme Court.[2]

Opponents charged that by annexing over 47,000 new residents (97 percent White), the White-dominated Richmond city council had sought to dilute growing Black political power.

Proponents argued that the annexation's value was based on strengthening Richmond's middle-class population, acquiring vacant land for residential, commercial, and industrial growth, and expanding the tax base to meet Richmond's future revenue needs

The irony is that both sides were correct. By unanimous vote, the U.S. Supreme Court ruled in 1975 that the annexation "was infected by the impermissible purpose of denying the right to vote based on race."[3] The Court allowed the annexation to stand,

---

power to the suburbs was under way. A failure of initiative from within as well as legal and historical constraints from without contributed to making many older cities inelastic.

By contrast, younger cities were cities "on the make" as they

based on Richmond's shift to a nine-member council elected by wards.

After adding 47,000 new residents (and an estimated one-quarter to its tax base), the 1970 annexation, however, marked the end of Richmond's expansion. Blacks gained a majority of the ward council seats by 1978, electing Henry Marsh as Richmond's first Black mayor.

Richmond's Black community has gained political control of a depreciating asset. While the three adjacent counties have almost doubled with 221,000 new residents, Richmond's population has dropped by 46,000, or −19 percent since 1970. City income growth has steadily lagged behind suburban income growth. City incomes are now 83 percent of suburban incomes. Richmond's Black middle class is beginning to leave the city for suburban locations.

Richmond's annexation powers were effectively ended by the Virginia legislature, which in 1979 exempted urban counties from further annexation without county approval. Probably Richmond's Black majority city council would have lost all interest in further annexations in any event in order not to jeopardize its newly acquired political power.

The saga of Richmond's annexation battle encapsulates one of urban America's sad realities. In many cities, achieving political dominance has also trapped many Blacks or Hispanics in cities of declining social and economic opportunity. Minority political control seems to accelerate abandonment of the city by middle-class residents, investors, and employers.

1. These statistics are compiled by the author from a report entitled "Complete Listing of Objections Pursuant to the Voting Rights Act of 1965," issued by the Department of Justice, Voting Rights Division (December 31, 1992). I have treated one submission of 525 annexations by one South Carolina city in 1986 as a single submission. (The Justice Department's objection to that annexation package was ultimately withdrawn.)
2. All information on the history of the Richmond annexation dispute is taken from John V. Moeser and Rutledge M. Dennis, *The Politics of Annexation: Oligarchic Power in a Southern City* (Cambridge, Mass.: Schenkman Publishing Company, 1982).
3. Ibid., 172.

entered the postwar era. Certainly, many would benefit from macroeconomic changes (for example, the growth of industry in the Sunbelt). Many would even benefit from microeconomic changes in technology (for example, inexpensive air conditioning units for Sunbelt homes and offices). But many cities made their own futures through adopting expansive policies. They made their own "elasticity."

Lesson 14: Racial prejudice has shaped growth patterns.

Racial patterns helped set the stage for the different postwar growth patterns in different regions. The Northeast and Midwest had few Blacks and even fewer Hispanics in their small towns and rural areas; minorities were almost exclusively located in larger cities.[10] The South had significant numbers of Blacks in rural counties, and the West had numerous Hispanics in southwestern towns. The outward expansion of many southern and western cities would not cross a racial boundary as markedly as in the Northeast and Midwest, though in some southern communities the politics of White domination could put a special spin on annexation issues (see Box 1.3).

TABLE 1.11
INELASTIC AREAS ARE MORE SEGREGATED THAN ELASTIC AREAS

Metro area	Percentage Black (1990)		Black segregation index
	Metro area	City	
Houston, Tex.	19%	27%	0.66
Detroit, Mich.	21	75	0.88
Columbus, Ohio	12	22	0.67
Cleveland, Ohio	19	46	0.85
Nashville, Tenn.	15	24	0.61
Louisville, Ky.	13	30	0.69
Indianapolis, Ind.	14	22	0.74
Milwaukee, Wis.	14	30	0.83
Albuquerque, N. Mex.	3	3	0.39
Syracuse, N.Y.	6	20	0.73
Madison, Wis.	3	4	0.48
Harrisburg, Pa.	7	50	0.76
Raleigh, N.C.	25	24	0.48
Richmond, Va.	29	55	0.59

Admittedly, some factors in suburban growth in the early postwar decades were nonracial. Many middle-class families became suburbanites because the older cities lacked dream houses at affordable prices in good neighborhoods with good schools. Others went to the suburbs to flee high city taxes and low city politics or to live nearer new, suburban-based jobs.

Yet in many metro areas, racially motivated "White flight" was undeniably a major factor in suburban growth. "Good" neighborhoods with "good" schools often were seen as neighborhoods and schools without any Blacks and, to a lesser degree, without any Hispanics. After the civil rights revolution in the 1960s, neighborhoods and schools without poor Blacks and Hispanics met the "good" test.

Racial prejudice played a role in the evolution of over-whelmingly White suburbs surrounding increasingly Black cities. How strong a role is debatable, but the demographic, social, and economic consequences have become clear over the past forty years.

Lesson 15: Inelastic areas are more segregated than elastic areas.

Today the high concentration of Blacks and Hispanics, particularly poor Blacks and Hispanics, within central cities of inelastic areas dominates their social geography and the choices that middle-class families (White and Black) must make about where to live and work. Table 1.11 illustrates the measurable differences between inelastic areas and elastic areas in terms of residential segregation of Blacks. (For an explanation of the index used, see Box 1.4.)

As stated earlier, each pair in our sample has similar percentages of Blacks in the population metrowide. The sharply different metro growth patterns yielded sharply different racial populations for central cities.

Metro Houston is 19 percent black. Many of its new "suburbs" are within its city limits. The city of Houston is only 27 percent Black. Metro Detroit has a slightly higher Black population (21 percent) than does Houston's metro area. With *all* of its new suburbs outside its city limits, however, the city of Detroit is 75 percent Black.

The metrowide residential segregation index for Blacks in the

---

Box 1.4 Census Bureau Calculates Residential Segregation

Building on the path-breaking work of sociologists Karl and Alma Taeuber, Douglas Massey, and Nancy Denton, the Census Bureau published a study of residential segregation in all 320 metro areas.[1] Using nineteen different statistical measures, the Census Bureau measured evenness, exposure, concentration, centralization, and clustering for Blacks, Hispanics, Asians, and American Indians. Calculations were conducted for all areas with Black, Hispanic, or Asian populations of 2 percent or more and of 1 percent or more American Indians.

Blacks are much more segregated than are Hispanics. Among large metro areas of 1 million or more people, the ten most segregated metro areas for Blacks are Detroit, Milwaukee, Cleveland, Newark, St. Louis, Chicago, Indianapolis, Philadelphia, New York, and Minneapolis–St. Paul. The least segregated large metro areas for Blacks are Middlesex-Somerset-Hunterdon, N.J., San Jose, Riverside–San Bernardino, Charlotte-Gastonia-Rock Hill, Norfolk–Virginia Beach–Newport News, San Diego, Phoenix, San Antonio, Nassau-Suffolk, Sacramento, and Seattle.

Throughout this book I have used the "Taeuber" or "dissimilarity index" as the sole measure of residential segregation. In effect, it measures "evenness"—what proportion of a minority population would have to move to produce an absolutely proportional distribution of that minority population across all census tracts of a metro area.

A dissimilarity index of 1.00 would indicate total segregation (that is, a completely uneven distribution of minorities); an index of 0.00 would indicate complete integration (that is, a completely even and uniform distribution of minorities).

1. Roderick J. Harrison and Daniel H. Weinberg, "Racial and Ethnic Segregation in 1990" (Washington, D.C.: U.S. Bureau of the Census, April 1992).

Houston metro area is 0.66; for Blacks in the Detroit metro area it is 0.88. (Complete segregation equals 1.00; complete integration equals 0.00.)

Racial segregation in inelastic areas is consistently high. Segregation of Blacks is always less within the elastic metro area in a pair than it is in the inelastic metro area. Between metro areas in different regions (for example, Houston-Detroit, Albuquerque-

Syracuse), differences in racial patterns might be explained in terms of broad regional differences (Sunbelt-Frostbelt, for example). The relationship, however, holds true between metro areas in the same region (Raleigh-Richmond, Nashville-Louisville) and even within the same state (Columbus-Cleveland).

Lesson 16: Inelastic areas that segregate Blacks segregate Hispanics.

Hispanics are significantly less segregated than are Blacks (although Hispanic segregation is growing in many areas). Typically, the level of Hispanic residential segregation is 0.20 to 0.30 points below Black segregation within the same metro area. In addition, southwestern communities tend to have many more Hispanics than do other areas of the country. In less elastic areas, however, even small Hispanic populations are usually highly segregated (Table 1.12).[11]

Lesson 17: City-suburb income gaps are more of a problem than overall income levels in metro areas.

The city-suburb per capita income ratio is the single most important indicator of an urban area's social health (Table 1.13). Income levels in inelastic cities fall well below suburban levels (Detroit and Cleveland, 53 percent). Elastic cities, however, keep pace with suburban levels (Houston, 89 percent, Nashville, 98 percent) or even exceed suburban levels (Raleigh, 103 percent, Albuquerque, 118 percent).

The city-suburb per capita income ratio is also an almost unerring barometer of a mayor's national politics. In May 1992 many of the nation's mayors marched on the Congress and White House to appeal for $35 billion in new federal aid to urban areas. The mayors of Detroit, Cleveland, Louisville, Milwaukee, Syracuse, Harrisburg, and Richmond supported the "Save Our Cities" appeal. The mayors of elastic cities within our sample (with the exception of Madison's mayor) did not. Yet the metro areas from which the supportive mayors came had the same income levels (an average $14,892 per capita) as did the metro areas of the nonsupportive mayors ($14,850).

TABLE 1.12
INELASTIC AREAS THAT SEGREGATE BLACKS
SEGREGATE HISPANICS

Metro area	Percentage Hispanic (1990)		Hispanic segregation index
	Metro area	City	
Houston, Tex.	21%	28%	0.49
Detroit, Mich.	2	3	(.54)[a]
Columbus, Ohio	1	1	(.32)
Cleveland, Ohio	2	5	(.68)
Nashville, Tenn.	1	1	(.42)
Louisville, Ky.	1	1	(.34)
Indianapolis, Ind.	1	1	(.43)
Milwaukee, Wis.	4	6	0.56
Albuquerque, N. Mex.	37	35	0.42
Syracuse, N.Y.	1	3	(.47)
Madison, Wis.	2	2	(.40)
Harrisburg, Pa.	2	8	(.68)
Raleigh, N.C.	1	1	(.41)
Richmond, Va.	1	1	N/A

[a]The Census Bureau study did not calculate indices of residential segregation of Hispanics in metro areas with less than a 2 percent Hispanic population. Because of the near identical relationship between Hispanic residential segregation and Hispanic school segregation, I have substituted Hispanic school segregation indices, where needed, from a study I conducted with the Urban Institute. These substitutions are indicated by parentheses.

The crux of the issue is the sharp disparities *within* the metro area. Inelastic cities had per capita incomes ($11,102) only 68 percent of suburban levels, while income levels within elastic cities ($14,634) were equal (96 percent) to suburban levels. As a result, income levels for elastic cities were 32 percent above income levels of inelastic cities, even though both sets of cities are located in areas of equal wealth.

Many mayors of inelastic cities go to Washington because they do not have the ability (or the inclination) to get their suburban neighbors to share the burden. They are trapped between having an ever smaller slice of the metro tax base and an ever growing share of metro social burdens.

Mayors of elastic cities, by contrast, find many of their "sub-

TABLE 1.13
CITY-SUBURBAN INCOME GAPS ARE MORE OF A PROBLEM
THAN METRO INCOME LEVELS

| Metro area | Per capita income (1989) | | | City-suburb ratio |
	Metro area	City	Suburb	
Houston, Tex.	$15,091	$14,261	$16,012	89%
Detroit, Mich.	15,694	9,443	17,874	53
Columbus, Ohio	14,516	13,151	16,169	81
Cleveland, Ohio	15,092	9,258	17,317	53
Nashville, Tenn.	14,567	14,490	14,808	98
Louisville, Ky.	13,600	11,527	14,564	79
Indianapolis, Ind.	15,159	14,478	16,120	90
Milwaukee, Wis.	14,785	11,106	17,868	62
Albuquerque, N. Mex.	13,594	14,018	11,892	118
Syracuse, N.Y.	13,918	11,351	17,868	77
Madison, Wis.	15,542	15,143	15,976	95
Harrisburg, Pa.	14,659	11,037	15,251	72
Raleigh, N.C.	16,170	16,896	16,377	103
Richmond, Va.	15,848	13,993	16,777	83

urbs'' within their own city limits. Their city revenue bases have expanded dramatically. Often city governments of elastic cities are better financed than are outlying jurisdictions. Poor minorities are not heavily concentrated within the central city. For cities that are expanding very aggressively, the ''suburbs'' outside the city limits are often poor rural and semirural areas. Under such conditions mayors usually choose to handle local problems with local revenues rather than seek federal urban aid.

Lesson 18: Fragmented local government fosters segregation; unified local government promotes integration.

The fragmentation of metro areas into multiple local governments is associated with the degree of residential segregation.

For most Americans, smaller is better and home rule is an unassailable democratic good. But the sad reality is that the

TABLE 1.14
FRAGMENTED LOCAL GOVERNMENT FOSTERS SEGREGATION;
UNIFIED LOCAL GOVERNMENT PROMOTES INTEGRATION

Metro area	Percentage of area population governed by central city	Number of suburban governments	Segregation index	
			Blacks	Hispanics
Houston, Tex.	49%	79	0.66	0.49
Detroit, Mich.	23	338	0.88	(.54)[a]
Columbus, Ohio	46	203	0.67	(.32)
Cleveland, Ohio	28	62	0.85	(.68)
Nashville, Tenn.	50	46	0.61	(.42)
Louisville, Ky.	28	163	0.69	(.34)
Indianapolis, Ind.	59	160	0.74	(.43)
Milwaukee, Wis.	44	93	0.83	0.56
Albuquerque, N. Mex.	80	3	0.39	0.42
Syracuse, N.Y.	25	97	0.73	(.47)
Madison, Wis.	52	59	0.48	(.40)
Harrisburg, Pa.	9	132	0.76	(.68)
Raleigh, N.C.	28	24	0.48	(.41)
Richmond, Va.	23	18	0.59	N/A

[a]The Census Bureau study did not calculate indices of residential segregation of Hispanics in metro areas with less than a 2 percent Hispanic population. Because of the near identical relationship between Hispanic residential segregation and Hispanic school segregation, I have substituted Hispanic school segregation indices, where needed, from a study I conducted with the Urban Institute. These substitutions are indicated by parentheses.

smaller the local jurisdiction or school district, the more narrow and exclusive the population served. In general, the more highly fragmented a metro area is, the more segregated it is racially and economically (Table 1.14). Smaller jurisdictions are typically organized to promote and protect uniformity rather than diversity. Conversely, areas characterized by geographically large, multipowered governments and more unified school systems tend to promote more racial and economic integration and achieve greater social mobility.

The critical issue is the number of different governments that control planning and zoning decisions. The key measures are the proportion of the metro area under the central city's control (column one in Table 1.14) and the number of suburban jurisdictions with planning and zoning powers (column two in Table 1.14). The final two columns repeat the indices of residential segregation explained in Box 1.3.

The way a metro area is governed is not the only factor affecting integration. Another factor is age. Old cities generally have more decaying neighborhoods in which poor Blacks and Hispanics are concentrated. Younger cities have emerged in an era of somewhat more enlightened racial attitudes (and some effective civil rights laws). In addition, regional racial patterns and overall economic trends affect the degree of integration.

Does greater socioeconomic integration automatically flow from greater governmental unity? Probably not. What is clear is that, absent federal or state mandates, a metro area in which local government is highly fragmented is usually incapable of adopting broad, integrating strategies. Conversely, a metro area in which key planning and zoning powers are concentrated under a dominant local government has the potential to implement policies to promote greater racial and economic integration if that government has the courage and vision to do so.

Lesson 19: Dispersed and fragmented public education is more segregated than centralized and unified public education.

Table 1.15 depicts patterns in public education that parallel patterns in local general government. Public education in inelastic areas is characterized by a single, but shrinking, central-city school system surrounded by multiple suburban systems. Suburban Syracuse has 35 school systems; suburban Cleveland, 53; and suburban Detroit, 116!

By contrast, in elastic areas a unified, central-city school system is typically as dominant as the expanding central city. The Nashville public schools, for example, enroll 44 percent of metro area public school students.

Several Sunbelt states (for example, Florida and North Carolina) have countywide unified school districts that serve all or many of the municipalities within them. For instance, the four-county Raleigh-Durham area has twenty municipalities but only ten school districts. The Albuquerque public schools, the

Box 1.5 School Segregation Parallels Residential Segregation, Except in South

School segregation closely tracks residential segregation, except in the South. With court-ordered desegregation plans in effect within typically large school systems, southern schools are more integrated than southern neighborhoods.

Prior to the Census Bureau study of residential segregation, The Urban Institute and I analyzed school segregation within all metro areas.

The basic data source for all researchers of residential segregation are annual reports submitted by the state education agencies to the U.S. Department of Education's National Center for Education Statistics. With funds from the National Urban League, my colleagues and I at the Urban Institute purchased computer tapes detailing public school districts and school enrollments by race and ethnicity for elementary and secondary schools for the 1989–90 school year.[1]

In analyzing school segregation I have used the same "Taeuber" or "dissimilarity index" used by the Census Bureau as one of the measures of residential segregation (see Box 1.3). The Census Bureau study analyzed the distribution of minority residents across all census tracts within each metro area. My study analyzed the distribution of minority students across all public high schools of all school districts within each metro area.

Of the largest metro areas of 1,000,000 or more residents, Black school segregation is highest in Detroit; Bergen-Passaic, New Jersey; Newark; Cleveland; Chicago; Cincinnati; Hartford; Philadelphia; Columbus, Ohio; and Milwaukee. The least segregated school systems for Blacks in large metro areas are Charlotte; Tampa–St. Petersburg-Clearwater; Anaheim–Santa Ana, California; Riverside–San Bernardino, California; San Jose; Orlando; San Antonio; Fort Lauderdale-Hollywood-Pompano Beach, Florida; Salt Lake City; and Middlesex-Somerset-Hunterdon, New Jersey.

1. The data are incomplete, however. Eight states annually have not submitted information: Georgia, Idaho, Maine, Missouri, Montana, South Dakota, Virginia, and Wyoming. Among metro areas of 1,000,000 or more people, missing state reports have prevented analysis of Washington, D.C.-Maryland-Virginia; Atlanta, Georgia; Kansas City, Missouri–Kansas; and St. Louis, Missouri–Illinois.

TABLE 1.15
DISPERSED AND FRAGMENTED PUBLIC EDUCATION IS MORE
SEGREGATED THAN CENTRALIZED AND UNIFIED
PUBLIC EDUCATION

Metro area	Percentage of metro area students enrolled in city schools	Number of suburban school districts	School segregation index Blacks	Hispanics
Houston, Tex.	29%	38	0.59	0.50
Detroit, Mich.	23	116	0.90	0.54
Columbus, Ohio	25	52	0.71	0.32
Cleveland, Ohio	24	53	0.79	0.68
Nashville, Tenn.	41	7	0.47	0.42
Louisville, Ky.	64	9	0.37	0.34
Indianapolis, Ind.	19	44	0.62	0.43
Milwaukee, Wis.	38	36	0.70	0.58
Albuquerque, N. Mex.	100	0	0.31	0.44
Syracuse, N.Y.	15	35	0.76	0.47
Madison, Wis.	44	15	0.51	0.40
Harrisburg, Pa.	9	23	0.82	0.68
Raleigh, N.C.	57	10	0.32	0.41
Richmond, Va.	15	12	N/A	N/A

twenty-fifth largest system in the nation, serves not only all of Albuquerque and surrounding Bernalillo County but nearby communities in an adjacent county as well.

Table 1.15 measures school segregation metrowide by the same "dissimilarity index" I used to measure residential segregation metrowide. (See Box 1.3 for an explanation of this index.) Elastic areas are much less segregated for Black students (0.50) than are inelastic areas (0.72). Despite typically much larger Hispanic populations in elastic areas, the pattern of lower segregation holds for Hispanic students in elastic areas (0.42) as compared with inelastic areas (0.60).

Skeptics may argue that most southern school systems have federal court-ordered desegregation plans in effect. This is quite true, but because these systems are often countywide, they typically link city and suburb. Middle-class Whites cannot flee to other public school systems. Desegregation in these areas has been more successful and more stable than in areas where school desegregation plans apply solely within a central-city school system. Such limited school desegregation efforts have often prompted White flight to private schools or suburban systems.

The biggest departure from the pattern of elastic-inelastic communities in Table 1.15 (Louisville) illustrates these observations. In 1975, by federal court order, the city of Louisville's school system was merged with the Jefferson County school system to create one countywide school system. Within this unified system an aggressive and successful program of both racial integration and school reform has been under way for twenty years. A high degree of racial integration in the schools (0.37 for Blacks) and limited White flight from the system have been the result. Although the city of Louisville's population has dropped precipitously, the population of the rest of Jefferson County outside Louisville has increased 20 percent since the school system merger.

Tables 1.14 and 1.15 show that for Blacks, elastic-area schools are more desegregated (0.50) than are elastic-area neighborhoods (0.58). In highly fragmented, inelastic metro areas, Black school segregation (0.79) almost perfectly mirrors Black neighborhood segregation (0.81).

Especially when buttressed by federal court orders, broad-based public school systems are integrating mechanisms for elastic areas, while fragmented school structures (which frustrate desegregation efforts) reinforce racial segregation in inelastic areas.

These patterns of local government suggest a second law of urban dynamics: *fragmentation divides; unification unites.* This second law is subject, perhaps, to greater "relativity." Anecdotal proof is easier to compile than constructing compelling statistical proof.

Lesson 20: The global economy sets the rules, but local areas can decide how to play the game.

I certainly would not argue that major economic changes are driven by urban development patterns. The "deindustrialization" of the American economy, for example, is the result primarily of global competition in manufacturing in recent decades, not the ways in which metro areas have developed.

Deindustrialization has affected urban areas very differently. Table 1.16 shows these effects during the 1973–88 period (when deindustrialization was already well advanced).

The inelastic cities reached maturity during the industrial age. Their metro areas in 1973 were more highly industrialized (25 percent) than were elastic metro areas (16 percent). Moreover, their industrial bases (particularly Detroit's, Cleveland's, and Milwaukee's) emphasized "smokestack industries"—steel, automobiles, and other metal trades. These industries were among those hardest hit by international competition. The loss of manufacturing jobs was catastrophic for Detroit, Cleveland, Louisville, and Milwaukee. Inelastic areas, however, did gain in overall employment (23 percent), although manufacturing employment dropped from 25 percent to 17 percent of all jobs.

Several elastic areas (Albuquerque, Madison, Raleigh) grew up largely during the postindustrial era. New products such as

TABLE 1.16
ELASTIC AREAS ADJUST BETTER TO ECONOMIC CHANGE
THAN INELASTIC AREAS

Metro area	Percentage of metro jobs in manufacturing		
	1973	1973–88	1988
Houston, Tex.	15%	3%	10%
Detroit, Mich.	32	−25	21
Columbus, Ohio	21	−14	13
Cleveland, Ohio	30	−29	20
Nashville, Tenn.	21	9	15
Louisville, Ky.	27	−26	17
Indianapolis, Ind.	23	−16	15
Milwaukee, Wis.	30	−17	21
Albuquerque, N. Mex.	9	51	7
Syracuse, N.Y.	22	−12	15
Madison, Wis.	10	48	10
Harrisburg, Pa.	21	−8	15
Raleigh, N.C.	15	58	13
Richmond, Va.	18	−5	12

computers and electronic components often characterized these metro areas' industrial activities. Albuquerque, Madison, and Raleigh built impressively on small manufacturing bases. Yet, except for Madison, manufacturing declined in importance in each of these elastic areas.

To test my thesis about elastic versus inelastic cities, it is best to examine metro areas within the same region or state. This minimizes Sunbelt-Frostbelt confusion. For example, while inelastic Louisville lost industrial jobs (-26 percent), elastic Nashville gained ($+9$ percent); while inelastic Richmond lost industrial jobs (-5 percent), elastic Raleigh gained ($+58$ percent).

More striking are the contrasts between areas that have both been caught up by deindustrialization. Both Columbus and Cleveland lost many manufacturing jobs, but elastic Columbus boomed while inelastic Cleveland stagnated. The percentage decline in manufacturing jobs was about the same in elastic Indianapolis and inelastic Milwaukee, but Indianapolis is clearly the more economically vigorous area.

Past prosperity may have lulled old industrial areas into complacency. Many have failed to tool up for economic change. The level of education of the labor force is a good measure of adaptability of areas to the postindustrial, information age. As shown in Table 1.17, the elastic areas boast higher percentages of workers with B.A. degrees or above (25 percent) than the inelastic areas (20 percent).[12]

Lesson 21: The smaller the income gap between city and suburb, the greater the economic progress for the whole metropolitan community.

The National League of Cities has released a widely reported study that concluded that, of forty-eight large metro areas, those with the smallest central city/suburban income gaps had the greatest job increases.[13]

Table 1.18 tests this observation for the pairs of metro areas. For inelastic areas the city-suburb income ratio was 68 percent; from 1973 to 1988 the overall growth in jobs was 23 percent. By contrast, in elastic areas (with a city-suburb income ratio of 96 percent) the fifteen-year growth in employment was 58 percent.

Job growth can be just a proxy for population growth. Are the lives of elastic area residents getting better compared with those of inelastic area residents? The answer is yes, although not as

TABLE 1.17
ELASTIC AREAS TEND TO HAVE A HIGHER EDUCATED WORK FORCE
THAN INELASTIC AREAS

Metro area	Percentage of metro area workers with B.A. degrees or above, 1990
Houston, Tex.	25%
Detroit, Mich.	18
Columbus, Ohio	23
Cleveland, Ohio	20
Nashville, Tenn.	21
Louisville, Ky.	17
Indianapolis, Ind.	21
Milwaukee, Wis.	21
Albuquerque, N. Mex.	27
Syracuse, N.Y.	22
Madison, Wis.	34
Harrisburg, Pa.	18
Raleigh, N.C.	25
Richmond, Va.	24

dramatically as the differential in employment growth. From 1969 to 1989, real per capita income in these elastic areas grew 41 percent compared with 30 percent in inelastic areas (Table 1.19). This growth occurred despite the decade-long collapse in oil and gas and real estate prices in the Southwest that severely depressed income growth in Houston and Albuquerque.

These observations lead to my third law of urban dynamics: *ties do bind.* Admittedly, the data are mixed. If this were a physics text, the third law might be described as a weak nuclear force. Can suburbs successfully create viable, self-contained suburban economies and abandon their central cities? Can America *afford* to bet on the answer?

Lesson 22: Poverty is more concentrated in inelastic cities than in elastic cities.

What about poverty levels? Historically, the South and West have been lower income regions than the Northeast and Midwest. That pattern still persists (Table 1.20). A slightly higher

TABLE 1.18
ELASTIC AREAS HAVE FASTER RATES OF JOB CREATION THAN
INELASTIC AREAS

Metro area	City-suburb per capita income rate ratio 1989	Metro job growth 1973–88
Houston, Tex.	89%	67%
Detroit, Mich.	53	11
Columbus, Ohio	81	40
Cleveland, Ohio	53	8
Nashville, Tenn.	98	55
Louisville, Ky.	79	21
Indianapolis, Ind.	90	34
Milwaukee, Wis.	62	22
Albuquerque, N. Mex.	118	75
Syracuse, N.Y.	77	27
Madison, Wis.	95	51
Harrisburg, Pa.	72	29
Raleigh, N.C.	103	81
Richmond, Va.	83	46

percentage of the population fell below the poverty line in southern and western areas (12 percent) than in northeastern and midwestern areas (10 percent) regardless of local metropolitan dynamics. However, poverty is much more concentrated in the inelastic cities (25 percent) than in the elastic cities (15 percent). In part, the pattern is regional. In the South and West, many poor households still live in rural and semiurban sections of the metro areas. Poverty is both more spread out in the countryside and more dispersed within the urbanized area itself. But concentrated poverty is also the result of cities' inelasticity, which magnifies economic segregation.

In determining the poverty threshold the same income standard is applied around the country, but the real cost of living varies. For the metro areas in my sample, the inelastic areas are about 5 to 10 percent more expensive to live in than are the elastic areas. For the same dollars, people are poorer in these inelastic areas than in these elastic areas. Elastic cities are home

TABLE 1.19
ELASTIC AREAS SHOW GREATER GAINS IN REAL INCOME THAN
INELASTIC AREAS

Metro area	Percentage growth in real per capita income in metro areas, 1969–89
Houston, Tex.	36%
Detroit, Mich.	26
Columbus, Ohio	34
Cleveland, Ohio	23
Nashville, Tenn.	49
Louisville, Ky.	30
Indianapolis, Ind.	32
Milwaukee, Wis.	25
Albuquerque, N. Mex.	41
Syracuse, N.Y.	29
Madison, Wis.	34
Harrisburg, Pa.	33
Raleigh, N.C.	62
Richmond, Va.	45

to only slightly more than their fair share of the metro area poor (index: 128). By contrast, inelastic cities must cope with too many poor people (index: 234).

As social tinder, poverty in elastic areas typically lacks the critical mass it has in the highly concentrated ghettos of inelastic cities of the Northeast and Midwest.

Lesson 23: Elastic cities have better bond ratings than inelastic cities.

City-suburb income disparities are further reflected in municipal bond markets. Bond rating agencies must assess the risk associated with a city government's debts. Ratings are based on long-term economic outlook and past debt management. The highest rating (AAA) indicates a blue-chip investment. The lowest municipal bond rating (B) is near the investment level of a junk bond.

The debt management of some inelastic cities (Milwaukee,

TABLE 1.20
POVERTY IS MORE CONCENTRATED IN INELASTIC CITIES THAN IN
ELASTIC CITIES

Metro area	Percentage of metro population below the poverty line, 1990	Percentage of city population below the poverty line, 1990	City's fair share index of metro area poor population, 1990
Houston, Tex.	15%	21%	137%
Detroit, Mich.	13	32	251
Columbus, Ohio	12	17	146
Cleveland, Ohio	12	29	243
Nashville, Tenn.	11	13	119
Louisville, Ky.	13	23	178
Indianapolis, Ind.	10	12	130
Milwaukee, Wis.	12	22	191
Albuquerque, N. Mex.	15	14	96
Syracuse, N.Y.	10	23	218
Madison, Wis.	10	16	153
Harrisburg, Pa.	8	27	346
Raleigh, N.C.	10	12	116
Richmond, Va.	10	21	213

Syracuse, Richmond) has been better than their social management (Table 1.21), but the patterns for elastic and inelastic cities
hold. The elastic cities averaged AA1 ratings. Inelastic cities averaged A1 ratings. Detroit, Cleveland, and Harrisburg are in
severe fiscal distress.

Finally, what is statistically clear if politically unacknowledge-
able is the last lesson that I draw from these past forty years of
urban America.

Lesson 24: Rebuilding inner cities from within has not happened.

After the riot last spring in South Central Los Angeles, the most
ominous news story I read detailed not what had just happened
in South Central Los Angeles but what had not happened in the

TABLE 1.21
ELASTIC CITIES HAVE BETTER BOND RATINGS THAN
INELASTIC CITIES

Metro area	City bond rating
Houston, Tex.	AA
Detroit, Mich.	BAA1
Columbus, Ohio	AA1
Cleveland, Ohio	BAA1
Nashville, Tenn.	AAA
Louisville, Ky.	A
Indianapolis, Ind.	AAA
Milwaukee, Wis.	AA
Albuquerque, N. Mex.	AA
Syracuse, N.Y.	AA
Madison, Wis.	AAA
Harrisburg, Pa.	BAA
Raleigh, N.C.	AAA
Richmond, Va.	AA

Watts section of Los Angeles in the twenty-seven years since the rioting there in 1965. Public and private efforts in Watts had not overcome continued economic and social decay. Indeed, successful clients of job training and other social programs moved out of Watts to better communities elsewhere in the Los Angeles area—a rational decision on their part.

It does not take riots to push inelastic cities into accelerated decline, although riots hasten the process. A combination of sustained population loss (20 percent or more), high minority population (30 percent or more), and a significant city-suburb income gap (70 percent or less) seems to define the point of no return for a central city.

Table 1.22 details the status of our paired cities regarding these three preconditions as of about 1980. The table also presents what has happened to the overall city population, percentage of minorities, and city-suburb income ratio in the decade since.

As a group the elastic cities continued to grow in population and basically maintained their parity in city-suburb income ra-

TABLE 1.22
IN INELASTIC CITIES, THE POPULATION CONTINUES TO DECLINE, THE MINORITY RATIO CONTINUES TO INCREASE, AND THE CITY-SUBURB INCOME GAP CONTINUES TO WIDEN

Metro area	Change in city population*		Percentage of minorities in city		City-suburb income ratio	
	By 1980	By 1990	1980	1990	1979	1989
Houston, Tex.	171%	174%	52%	58%	95%	89%
Detroit, Mich.	-35	-44	71	79	66	53
Columbus, Ohio	50	68	25	25	85	81
Cleveland, Ohio	-37	-45	50	53	63	53
Nashville, Tenn.	161	180	26	27	102	98
Louisville, Ky.	-19	-31	30	31	84	79
Indianapolis, Ind.	64	71	24	24	95	90
Milwaukee, Wis.	0	-15	36	39	82	62
Albuquerque, N. Mex.	244	297	41	42	124	118
Syracuse, N.Y.	-23	-26	24	26	87	77
Madison, Wis.	92	99	10	10	98	95
Harrisburg, Pa.	-41	-42	55	59	82	72
Raleigh, N.C.	139	217	38	39	102	103
Richmond, Va.	-5	-19	54	57	90	85

*Population changes are measured either from 1950 or a city's peak population after 1950.

tio, while increasing only slightly the percentage of minorities (from 31 percent to 32 percent). Inelastic cities, however, continued to slide downward on all counts. During the decade, the overall population fell further from earlier peaks, the city-suburb income gap widened (from 79 percent to 69 percent), and the minority population increased from 46 percent to 49 percent—almost three times the rate of increase of the elastic cities.

Of our sample inelastic cities only Detroit and Cleveland had dropped below all three critical levels, although all the others were moving in that direction. This inexorable downward trend of inelastic cities suggests the fourth law of urban dynamics: *ghettos can only become bigger ghettos.*

Conclusion

Looking back over all the lessons learned, what composite profile can be drawn for inelastic and elastic areas?

An inelastic area has a central city frozen within its city limits and surrounded by growing suburbs. It may have a strong downtown business district as a regional employment center, but its city neighborhoods are increasingly catch basins for poor Blacks and Hispanics. With the flight of middle-class families, the city's population has dropped steadily (typically by 20 percent or more). The income gap between city residents and suburbanites steadily widens. City government is squeezed between rising service needs and eroding incomes. Unable to tap the areas of greater economic growth (its suburbs) the city becomes increasingly reliant on federal and state aid. The suburbs are typically fragmented into multiple towns and small cities and mini school systems. This very fragmentation of local government reinforces racial and economic segregation. Rivalry among jurisdictions often inhibits the whole area's ability to respond to economic challenges.

In an elastic area suburban subdivisions expand around the central city, but the central city is able to expand as well and capture much of that suburban growth within its municipal boundaries. Although no community is free of racial inequities, minorities are more evenly spread throughout the area. Segregation by race and income class is reduced. City incomes are typically equal to or higher than suburban incomes. Tapping a broader tax base, an elastic city government is better financed and more inclined to rely on local resources to address local problems. In fact, local public institutions, in general, tend to be more unified and promote more united and effective responses to economic challenges.

Notes

1. The 1950 census did not identify Hispanics as either a racial or ethnic group (aside from about 600,000 foreign-born Hispanics of Mexican and other Latin American origin). I have adopted an estimate of about 4 million Hispanics in 1950.

2. A majority of all Blacks live in metropolitan New York, Chicago, Los Angeles, Philadelphia, Detroit, Atlanta, Houston, Baltimore, Miami, Dallas–Fort Worth, San Francisco, Oakland, Cleveland, New Orleans, St. Louis, Memphis, Norfolk–Virginia Beach–Newport News, Richmond–Petersburg, Birmingham, Charlotte, Milwaukee, Cincinnati, Kansas City, Tampa–St. Petersburg–Clearwater, and Washington, D.C. Adding San Antonio, San Diego, El Paso, and San Jose to these metro areas accounts for a majority of all Hispanics. Adding Honolulu covers a majority of all Asians.

3. In 1790 the national population density was 4.5 persons per square mile. In 1990 for a country four times as large in area (including Alaska), the national population density was 70.3 persons per square mile.

4. For the 193 central cities identified as such in the 1950 census, the average density was 7,517 persons per square mile.

5. I do not mean "upward" literally—that is, through high-rise development—but through low-density, in-fill development. A low-density city's population density, in effect, can move upward.

6. The designation of "elastic" or "inelastic" is always based on the characteristics of a central city. Although a metro area also will be referred to as an elastic area or inelastic area, that qualifier reflects its central city's status.

7. Among 320 metro areas the only exceptions are New York City, Pittsburgh, Jersey City, St. Joseph (Missouri), and eight mining industry regions.

8. Examples are Baltimore, Philadelphia, San Francisco, and St. Louis. Virginia's "independent cities" had strong annexation powers until 1979 when the legislature placed, in effect, a moratorium on further annexation.

9. In Table 1.9, Davidson and Marion counties' negative growth "outside the city" reflects the incorporation of existing residents into the new consolidated governments of Nashville-Davidson and Indianapolis-Marion County.

10. Until ratification of the Fourteenth Amendment to the U.S. Constitution in 1868, some northeastern and midwestern states had Black exclusion laws. One example is Indiana.

12. Indeed, the presence of a major, high-quality university is often an engine supporting local, postindustrial growth. Between our two sample groups the major universities in elastic areas are Houston-Rice, Ohio State, Vanderbilt, Indiana (Indianapolis campus), New Mexico, Wisconsin, and the Research Tri-

angle's Duke–North Carolina–North Carolina State. Major universities in inelastic areas are Wayne State, Cleveland State–Case Western Reserve, Louisville, Marquette-Wisconsin (Milwaukee campus), Syracuse, Dickinson College, and Virginia Commonwealth–Richmond.

13. William R. Barnes and Larry C. Ledebur. *City Distress, Metropolitan Disparities, and Economic Growth.* Washington, D.C., National League of Cities, September 1992.

Chapter II

Characteristics of Metropolitan Areas

How does this concept of city elasticity affect demographic, social, and economic patterns of all cities and metro areas beyond those examined in chapter I? To analyze this phenomenon I have constructed an "elasticity score" for the 522 central cities in the nation's 320 Metropolitan Statistical Areas.

The 320 metro areas in America range in population from Los Angeles (8,863,164) to Enid, Oklahoma (56,735). Lumping areas of such disparate size into common categories produces "averages" that hide more than they reveal. Therefore, I will exclude from further analysis the lowest end of the scale—the 131 metro areas with fewer than 200,000 residents in 1990.[1] Of the 189 remaining metro areas, four other groups seem to march to a different drummer. For the following reasons these also are being excluded from my proposed categories.

First, I exclude three "Mexican border towns": El Paso, McAllen-Edinburg-Mission, and Brownsville-Harlingen. Along with Laredo, a smaller metro area, these Texas communities sit on the northern bank of the Rio Grande opposite major Mexican communities. With high resident populations of Hispanics (70 percent to 94 percent) and thousands of Mexican workers and shoppers commuting daily across the border, these Texas cities are really economic and sociological extensions of northern Mexico.

Second, I exclude five "declining mining regions," along with six smaller areas. These regions have lost population and wealth because of the decades-long decline of coal mining in West Virginia and Appalachian Pennsylvania, Ohio, and Maryland, and of iron ore mining around Duluth, Minnesota, and Superior, Wisconsin. Their central cities have lost population and wealth as well.[2]

51

Third, I exclude from further analysis thirteen "White-only metro areas." These thirteen areas have few Blacks (0.9 percent) and few Hispanics (2.4 percent). Their small Black and Hispanic communities seem to be exposed "only" to minimal-to-moderate levels of residential and school segregation. Once again, including these areas in the larger analysis would distort the averages of the categories.[3]

The last group—"city-less metro areas"—is set apart for a purely technical reason. This group is composed of the three larger metro areas that the federal government has designated without central cities within their boundaries. To these three I have added two smaller, city-less metro areas. All are subunits of Consolidated Metropolitan Statistical Areas (CMSAs). They are Brazoria County, Texas (greater Houston); Beaver County, Pennsylvania (greater Pittsburgh); and Nassau-Suffolk counties, New York; Orange County, New York; and Monmouth-Ocean Counties, New Jersey (all in greater New York). Within these areas, employment locations are highly dispersed; their real central cities, of course, are Houston, Pittsburgh, and New York City.

After excluding all of the above, I have 165 metro areas for further categorization. The range of characteristics is still wide: in metro population, from Los Angeles (8,863,164) to Gainesville, Florida (204,111); in municipal area, from Anchorage, Alaska, (1,698 square miles) to York, Pennsylvania (5 square miles); in metro per capita income, from Fairfield County, Connecticut ($26,161) to Visalia-Tulare-Porterville, California ($9,318); in Black population metrowide, from Jackson, Mississippi (42 percent) to Boulder-Longmont, Colorado (0.8 percent); in Hispanic population metrowide, from Corpus Christi, Texas (52 percent) to Birmingham, Alabama (0.4 percent).

To cut down the variation, I have separated metro areas with principal central cities under 100,000 population from metro areas with principal central cities over 100,000 population. In trying to classify all these areas coherently, I have not excluded any from my initial analysis. I have applied the same elasticity criteria to all 320 metro areas and 522 central cities.

Among the 117 major metro areas with principal central cities above 100,000 population, the range of characteristics is still wide. Therefore, a lot of emphasis should not be placed by readers on summarizing the characteristics of different categories. The most telling tests of my point of view—the effects of

TABLE 2.1
SUMMARY OF CATEGORIES

Category	Large metro areas	Small metro areas	Total metro areas
Mexican border towns	3	1	4
Declining mining regions	5	6	11
White-only metro areas	13	0	13
City-less metro areas	3	2	5
Large central cities (100,000+ residents)	117	0	117
Smaller central cities (fewer than 100,000 residents)	48	0	48
Smallest central cities	0	122	122
TOTAL	189	131	320

urban elasticity and inelasticity—are comparisons of cities within the same region, state, or even metro area.

The results are summarized in Table 2.1. All 522 central cities are categorized by relative elasticity in Appendix A. The elasticity score represents the combined effect of a city's density (population per square mile) in 1950 and the degree to which it expanded its city limits between 1950 and 1990. Each city's initial density and degree of boundary expansion (by percentage) are ranked against those of all other cities in its group. A city's relative rankings (organized by decile) for the two key characteristics (initial density and boundary expansion) are multiplied together to produce a composite elasticity score.

New York City ranks in the lowest decile (1) for having one of the highest population densities in 1950 (25,046 per square mile). It also ranks in the lowest decile (1) for not expanding its city limits at all. Therefore, New York City's elasticity score is 1 (1 × 1). Anchorage, Alaska, ranks in the next to highest decile (9) for having among the lowest population densities in 1950 (3,539 per square mile). It ranks in the highest decile (10) for having one of the highest boundary expansion rates (13,482 percent). Therefore, Anchorage's elasticity score is an almost perfect 90 (9 × 10).

I have ranked all cities by their elasticity scores into deciles and split them into five groupings: zero elasticity, low elasticity, medium elasticity, high elasticity, and hyper elasticity. (New

---

Box 2.1 Whatever Happened to the City of Spring Garden?

What ever happened to Spring Garden, Northern Liberties, Kensington, Southwark, and Moyamensing? In 1850 these Pennsylvania communities were the ninth, eleventh, twelfth, twentieth, and twenty-eighth most populous cities in America! Four years later they were annexed to the larger city of Philadelphia to frame the boundaries of Philadelphia substantially as we know it today.

In fact, ten of the country's fifty largest cities in 1850 disappeared before 1900. They all were consolidated into larger governmental bodies.

In 1867 Boston annexed the city of Roxbury; seven years later it leaped across Boston Harbor to annex the city of Charlestown. Allegheny in 1907 was taken in by Pittsburgh. And in the tradition of "little fish-big fish-bigger fish," the twenty-fourth largest city in 1850, Williamsburgh, was annexed in 1854 by the city of Brooklyn (seventh largest), which in turn became part of New York City in 1898 (see Box 1.2).

The political geography of old metropolitan areas may appear immutable to their residents today, but a century ago compelling public interests were served by such consolidations. Popular opposition as well as natural obstacles (harbors and rivers) had to be overcome, but the effort was worthwhile. These new governmental structures served their communities well for many decades.

York City is at the bottom of the zero-elasticity group; Anchorage leads the hyper-elasticity group.) The 117 largest areas are ranked in ascending order of elasticity (Table 2.2).[4]

The zero-elasticity group includes five inelastic cities described in Chapter I (Detroit, Cleveland, Louisville, Milwaukee, and Syracuse). It also includes New York, St Louis, Pittsburgh, Newark, Philadelphia, Baltimore, Miami, and Washington, D.C.—regular tenants of most lists of troubled cities. In addition, the zero-elasticity group includes cities conventionally viewed to be in good shape (for example, Boston, San Francisco, and Minneapolis–St. Paul).

The nineteen-member low-elasticity group includes Los Angeles, Atlanta, Seattle, Norfolk, New Orleans, Honolulu, and

Columbus. It is surprising to find both Los Angeles and Columbus as low-elasticity cities. Low-density Los Angeles, relying on extensive in-fill development, has expanded its city limits
very little since 1950. By contrast, Columbus, relatively high
density in 1950, has expanded its boundaries significantly.

Indianapolis, Nashville, Madison, and Richmond are among
the twenty-five members of the medium-elasticity group.
Others include Portland, Sacramento, Denver, Charlotte, An-
aheim, Kansas City, and Tampa. High-elasticity cities include
Albuquerque, Raleigh, Phoenix, San Antonio, Jacksonville,
Riverside, Fresno, Dallas, and San Jose. Albuquerque and San
Jose barely missed inclusion in the hyper-elasticity group, which
has among its members Houston, San Diego, Fort Worth, Las
Vegas, Oklahoma City, Tucson, and Austin.

A similar analysis has been applied to the 48 metro areas with
principal central cities under 100,000 (Harrisburg is a low-elasticity member of this category) as well as to the 131 smaller metro
areas.

Table 2.3 summarizes the average population growth of the
metro areas in each group. The zero-elasticity group began and
ended with the largest average metro population and experienced the lowest rate of metro population growth (35 percent).[5]
The other groups doubled or tripled their populations. Growth
rates, however important, should not be allowed to obscure the
fact that all groups, including the zero-elasticity group, added
an average of 500,000 to 650,000 residents between 1950 and
1990.

Table 2.4 demonstrates the dramatically different picture
among central cities. The thirty zero-elasticity cities all lost
population (an average loss of 21 percent) except for Paterson,
New Jersey, and Miami, which gained population by 1 percent
and 44 percent, respectively. Both are areas with many Hispanic
immigrants.

Although low-elasticity cities as a group gained in population
(31 percent), six cities of this group had fewer residents in 1990
than they had in 1950.[6] Most importantly, fifteen of the nineteen
low-elasticity cities have lost population since peaking out
sometime after 1950.[7]

Similarly, among the twenty-five medium-elasticity cities
(which gained 52 percent overall), between 1950 and 1990 there
were five net-population losers.[8] Eight more cities declined from

TABLE 2.2
117 MAJOR METRO AREAS GROUPED BY RELATIVE ELASTICITY

Zero Elasticity	Low Elasticity	Medium Elasticity	High Elasticity	Hyper Elasticity
New York* N.Y.	Honolulu* Hawaii	Richmond* Va.	Riverside, Calif.	Santa Rosa, Calif.
Newark* N.J.	Tacoma* Wash.	South Bend* Ind.	Fort Lauderdale, Fla.	Fort Worth* Tex.
Boston* Mass.	New Orleans* La.	Portland* Oreg.	Baton Rouge* La.	San Diego* Calif.
St Louis* Mo.	Dayton* Ohio	Lansing* Mich.	Memphis* Tenn.	Corpus Christi* Tex.
Detroit* Mich.	Allentown* Pa.	Lexington* Ky.	Lincoln* Nebr.	Houston* Tex.
Washington* D.C.	Erie* Pa.	Ann Arbor, Mich.	Stockton* Calif.	Jackson* Miss.
Pittsburgh* Pa.	Seattle* Wash.	Sacramento* Calif.	San Antonio* Tex.	Little Rock* Ark.
Cleveland* Ohio	Grand Rapids* Mich.	Rockford* Ill.	Columbus* Ga.	Vallejo, Calif.
San Francisco* Calif.	Norfolk* Va.	Denver* Colo.	Jacksonville* Fla.	Huntsville, Ala.
Paterson, N.J.	Peoria* Ill.	Omaha* Nebr.	Phoenix* Ariz.	Las Vegas, Nev.
Philadelphia* Pa.	Los Angeles* Calif.	Gary, Ind.	Shreveport* La.	Lubbock* Tex.
Buffalo* N.Y.	Atlanta* Ga.	Des Moines* Iowa	Salinas, Calif.	Reno, Nev.
Providence* R.I.	Savannah* Ga.	Charlotte* N.C.	Beaumont* Tex.	Greensboro* N.C.

Baltimore* Md.
Hartford* Conn.
Minneapolis* Minn.
Rochester* N.Y.
Syracuse* N.Y.
Jersey City* N.J.
Chicago* Ill.
Albany* N.Y.
Bridgeport* Conn.
Milwaukee* Wis.
New Haven* Conn.
Miami* Fla.
Oakland* Calif.
Worcester* Mass.
Springfield* Mass.
Louisville* Ky.
Cincinnati* Ohio

Flint† Mich.
Toledo* Ohio
Evansville* Ind.
Columbus* Ohio
Akron* Ohio
Fort Wayne* Ind.

Indianapolis* Ind.
Anaheim, Calif.
Oxnard, Calif.
Birmingham* Ala.
Nashville* Tenn.
Wichita* Kans.
Madison* Wis.
Kansas City* Mo.
Macon* Ga.
Knoxville* Tenn.
Tampa* Fla.
Tulsa* Okla.

Fresno* Calif.
Raleigh* N.C.
Dallas* Tex.
Modesto, Calif.
Mobile* Ala.
Chattanooga* Tenn.
Albuquerque* N. Mex.
San Jose* Calif.

Orlando* Fla.
Montgomery* Ala.
Tallahassee, Fla.
Oklahoma City* Okla.
Bakersfield, Calif.
Tucson, Ariz.
Colorado Springs, Colo.
Austin* Tex.
Anchorage, Alaska

An asterisk (*) indicates that the city was identified as a central city in the 1950 census.

Box 2.2 Hartford and Boston: Elasticity within Metro Areas

Within the same metro areas, the elasticity of cities differs. Elasticity helps determine the demographic, economic, and social characteristics of a city's future. Let us look within two metro areas: Harford and Boston.

Over the past forty years the Hartford metro area's population grew 72 percent. It is the country's thirteenth most prosperous metro area, and it has a relatively small Black population metro-wide (8 percent). City elasticities are strictly a function of the level of prior development. Political boundaries are fixed. In 1950 Hartford was a high-density city; New Britain, average density; and Middletown and Bristol, low density.

City	City elasticity score	City population 1950–90	City-suburb income ratio	City percentage Black
Hartford	*2	−21%	53%	36%
New Britain	3	2	70	7
Middletown	10	44	85	11
Bristol	18	69	81	2

*The elasticity for this city was scored within the group of larger cities (100,000 or more residents). The elasticity for the other cities in the table was scored among the smaller cities (fewer than 100,000 residents) for major metro areas.

The Boston area was America's oldest metropolis. Since 1950 the Boston area's population grew 23 percent. Up through 1989 the area continued to prosper, becoming the country's fifteenth wealthiest metro area. Its Black population was almost 6 percent

post-1950 population peaks.[9] Clearly, when a city stops growing, it starts shrinking.

Among the forty-three high-elasticity and hyper-elasticity cities, none lost population between 1950 and 1990, and only a handful may be peaking out.[10]

The combined effect of both trends is depicted in Table 2.5.

The zero-elasticity group had the largest average number of new-home buyers up for grabs among competing jurisdictions—760,000 persons (about half that group's average metro population in 1950). The low-elasticity group had the second largest number of new-home buyers—669,000 (slightly more than their

metrowide. In Massachusetts, as in Connecticut, the political map is fixed so that differences in elasticity are a function of differences in initial density of development.

City	City elasticity score	City population, 1950–90	City-suburb income ratio	City percentage Black
Boston	1*	−28%	77%	24%
Cambridge	2	−21	98	13
Lynn	3	−19	64	7
Lawrence	3	−13	48	2
Salem	6	−9	80	2
Lowell	6*	6	63	2
Waltham	12	23	83	3
Brockton	16	48	66	12
Haverhill	27	9	76	2
Framingham	27	46	101	3
Gloucester	30	14	79	0

*The elasticity for these cities was scored within the group of larger cities (100,000 or more residents). The elasticity for the other cities in the table was scored among the smaller cities (fewer than 100,000 residents) for major metro areas.

The patterns noted between elastic and inelastic cities at regional and state levels hold within the same metro areas. Inelastic cities lose population, develop sharp income gaps between city and suburb, and become more minority. Elastic cities gain population, generally maintain better income position, and tend to concentrate minorities less.

TABLE 2.3
ALMOST ALL METRO AREAS HAVE GROWN

Metro Area	Average metro population		Percentage change 1950–90
	1950	1990	
Zero-Elasticity	1,589,942	2,144,937	35%
Low-Elasticity	640,308	1,296,479	102
Medium-Elasticity	385,846	875,435	127
High-Elasticity	292,750	899,473	207
Hyper-Elasticity	234,713	763,753	225

TABLE 2.4
SOME CENTRAL CITIES HAVE GROWN; OTHERS HAVE SHRUNK

City	Average city population		Percentage change, 1950–90
	1950	1990	
Zero-Elasticity	904,590	712,075	−21%
Low-Elasticity	327,046	429,516	31
Medium-Elasticity	183,027	278,788	52
High-Elasticity	136,644	381,573	179
Hyper-Elasticity	112,763	338,063	200

average metro population in 1950). For the remaining groups the ratio of new-home buyers to average 1950 metro population continues to scale upward proportionally. All metro areas, however, had many new-home buyers for city and suburbs to compete over.

Table 2.6 illustrates the average population density in 1950 of central cities in each group. At 12,720 persons per square mile (217 percent of the national average of 5,873 persons per square mile), the zero-elasticity cities had little vacant land for new, low-density subdivision development; they had no alternative but to expand their boundaries. The low-elasticity cities and medium-elasticity cities were also above the national average. But the high-elasticity and hyper-elasticity cities had room to grow internally—although they would expand their boundaries dramatically as well.

Table 2.7 demonstrates that double-barrelled advantage. The zero-elasticity cities barely expanded their city limits (6 percent); of the thirty zero-elasticity cities, twelve did not expand their

TABLE 2.5
ALL GROUPS HAD ABOUT THE SAME NUMBER OF
NEW-HOME BUYERS

Metro Area	New-Home Buyers, 1950–90
Zero-Elasticity	760,818
Low-Elasticity	669,486
Medium-Elasticity	496,216
High-Elasticity	606,723
Hyper-Elasticity	529,040

TABLE 2.6
HIGH- AND HYPER-ELASTICITY CITIES CAN GROW THROUGH
IN-FILL; LOWER ELASTICITY CITIES CANNOT

City	City density (persons per square miles), 1950	City density as a percentage of the national average, 1950
Zero-Elasticity	12,720	217%
Low-Elasticity	6,691	114
Medium-Elasticity	6,132	104
High-Elasticity	4,549	77
Hyper-Elasticity	3,937	67

boundaries at all. The low-elasticity cities expanded modestly (44 percent), but the medium-, high-, and hyper-elasticity cities spread far and wide across the landscape.

By 1990 the average zero-elasticity city was the smallest in geographic area (sixty-four square miles), although the group covered a wide range in municipal size—from Paterson, New Jersey (eight square miles) to New York City (309 square miles). By contrast, the average high- or hyper-elasticity city was three or four times as large geographically. Within these latter groups the smallest cities in area were Salinas, Modesto, and Vallejo, California (eighteen, thirty, and thirty-one square miles, respectively).

The demographic payoff is summed up in Table 2.8 which shows each group's relative "capture/contribute" ratio. Zero-elasticity cities contributed −25 percent of their area's new-

TABLE 2.7
ELASTIC CITIES EXPAND THEIR CITY LIMITS;
INELASTIC CITIES DO NOT

City	City area (square miles) 1950	City area (square miles) 1990	Percentage change 1950–90
Zero-Elasticity	61	64	6%
Low-Elasticity	64	93	44
Medium-Elasticity	32	129	306
High-Elasticity	33	170	421
Hyper-Elasticity	33	240	625

TABLE 2.8
ELASTIC CITIES "CAPTURE" SUBURBAN GROWTH; INELASTIC CITIES
ONLY "CONTRIBUTE" TO SUBURBAN GROWTH

Area/City	City population change 1950–90	Metro new-home buyers 1950–90	City capture/ contribute percentage
Zero-Elasticity	−191,409	760,818	−25%
Low-Elasticity	102,469	669,486	15
Medium-Elasticity	95,761	496,216	19
High-Elasticity	244,929	606,723	40
Hyper-Elasticity	225,300	529,040	43

home buyers, while low-elasticity cities and medium-elasticity cities captured a modest 15 percent and 19 percent, respectively. High-elasticity cities and hyper-elasticity cities captured major chunks of suburban growth (40 and 43 percent, respectively). Zero-elasticity cities are the victims of their suburbs, but high- and hyper-elasticity cities often *are* their own suburbs.

Thus, an examination of the 117 major metro areas testifies again to the first law of urban dynamics: only elastic cities grow.

The social and economic consequences of these striking differences in city-suburb relationships are illustrated in the next tables. Table 2.9 shows that all groups have roughly the same percentage of Black residents metrowide (from 11 percent to 16 percent). The racial profile of central cities, however, differs substantially.

Hyper-elasticity and zero-elasticity cities are located in metro areas with the same proportional population of Blacks (13 per-

TABLE 2.9
INELASTIC AREAS ARE MORE SEGREGATED THAN ELASTIC AREAS

Area/City	Percentage Black, 1990		Black segregation index
	Metro	City	
Zero-Elasticity	13%	33%	0.72
Low-Elasticity	13	26	0.65
Medium-Elasticity	11	22	0.63
High-Elasticity	16	21	0.57
Hyper-Elasticity	13	18	0.57

cent). Because of the high concentration of Blacks within the inner city and their substantial exclusion from the suburbs, zero-elasticity cities are 33 percent Black, and their metrowide Black segregation index is a very high 0.72.

By contrast, hyper-elasticity cities embrace so much of their own suburban development that the proportion of Blacks in the city (18 percent) is not that much higher than the percentage metrowide. On a metrowide basis the index of Black segregation at a census tract or neighborhood level is 0.57 (significantly lower but still unacceptable).

Hispanic concentration and residential segregation follow similar patterns (Table 2.10) although the degree of residential segregation is measurably less for Hispanics than for Blacks.[11] The higher presence of Hispanics metrowide in high- and hyper-elasticity areas (14 percent and 13 percent, respectively) reflects the high degree to which cities in this group are located in California, Florida, and the Southwest—all areas of high Hispanic population.

Economic disparities flow in the same patterns. Table 2.11 analyzes patterns in per capita income among the groups. Zero-elasticity areas have the highest average suburban income ($18,435) and the lowest average city income ($12,728); the city-suburb income ratio is 71 percent. By contrast, hyper-elasticity areas have the second lowest average suburban income ($14,166) and the highest average city income ($14,390); the city-suburb income ratio is 104 percent.

In Chapter I, I presented several explanations for these disparities in racial and income distribution. I will now review them in the context of this broader analysis.

TABLE 2.10
INELASTIC AREAS THAT SEGREGATE BLACKS
SEGREGATE HISPANICS

Area/City	Percentage Hispanic, 1990		Hispanic Segregation Index
	Metro	City	
Zero-Elasticity	8%	13%	0.57
Low-Elasticity	4	5	0.37
Medium-Elasticity	5	8	0.40
High-Elasticity	14	16	0.42
Hyper-Elasticity	13	13	0.37

Box 2.3 Montgomery County: Unified Government Unites

Montgomery County, Maryland, is an outstanding example of the progress toward social and economic integration that can be achieved by a unified local government with both the authority and the political will to pursue such goals.

A wealthy suburban county outside Washington, D.C., Montgomery County grew from 164,401 residents in 1950 to 757,027 in 1990, surpassing the nation's capital. The area was a prime candidate for typical suburban balkanization. It did not happen for two reasons.

First, under Maryland state law, the county maintains a single, unified, countywide school system. With 102,385 students in 1991–92, the Montgomery County public schools are the nation's seventeenth largest school system—and clearly one of the best.

Second, in a far-sighted action the Maryland legislature in 1927 (revised in 1939) set up the Maryland–National Capital Park and Planning Commission and gave the Montgomery County government exclusive planning and zoning control throughout the county.[1] This legislative action created "a big enough canvas to work on," Richard Tustian, long-time county planner, once told me. This led to perhaps the nation's most comprehensive growth management system.

Most remarkable is the county's Moderately Priced Dwelling Unit (MPDU) Ordinance. First adopted in 1973, the policy requires builders of fifty or more residential units to set aside between 12.5 and 15 percent of the units for low- and moderate-income tenants or buyers. To compensate developers for providing housing below market prices, the county allows a density increase or "MPDU bonus" up to 22 percent above the normal density for the zone.

TABLE 2.11

CITY-SUBURB INCOME GAPS ARE MORE CRITICAL THAN OVERALL
METRO INCOME LEVELS

Area/City	Per capita income, 1989			City-suburb ratio
	Metro	City	Suburb	
Zero-Elasticity	$16,425	$12,728	$18,435	71%
Low-Elasticity	14,313	12,998	15,222	86
Medium-Elasticity	14,888	13,814	15,461	91
High-Elasticity	13,713	13,505	14,137	98
Hyper-Elasticity	14,331	14,390	14,166	104

Both buyers and renters are subject to maximum income limits set by the County Department of Housing and Community Development. Rent limits are controlled for twenty years. Sale and resale prices for MPDUs are controlled for ten years, and a portion of resale profits is recaptured by the county's revolving Housing Initiative Fund.

MPDUs must be sold to individual purchasers. Some, however, may be purchased by the Housing Opportunities Commission or a nonprofit organization for rent to low- and moderate-income households. By 1992 more than 9,500 housing units had been created under the policy.

The MPDU program has helped the county accommodate—and has even encouraged—a remarkable social transformation. In 1970 Montgomery County had the look of a classic suburb—wealthy and White (92 percent). By 1990 Montgomery County had a "rainbow" look—12 percent Black, 7 percent Hispanic, 8 percent Asian. Although Montgomery County is one of the country's richest urban counties, it also has a rich diversity of income groups.

Montgomery County's critics can point to unresolved social problems. But through the decades the Montgomery County government and Montgomery County public schools have demonstrated the ability of broad-based governments to resist the short-term, exclusive "Not-in-My-Backyard" syndrome and to act in the long-term interest of the larger community.

1. The legislature "grandfathered" existing zoning powers for the cities of Rockville and Gaithersburg and five small villages (about 12 percent of the county's population).

First, differences in racial and economic segregation are not related to the proportion of Blacks and Hispanics in an area. Areas with high proportions of minorities may be highly segregated or quite well integrated. Similarly, areas with low proportions of minorities may find minorities well blended into the larger community or highly isolated.

Second, although the proportion of minorities metrowide seems to have little to do with the degree of racial segregation, the historic distribution, or racial profile, plays some role. Traditionally, Blacks and Hispanics have lived in rural and small-town areas in the South and West but not in the Northeast and Midwest. As urbanization has reached into the countryside, southern and western cities have not encountered as sharp "racial gradients" as have northeastern and midwestern cities.

Third, the absolute size of the metro area has little effect on the racial and economic isolation of city dwellers. Some of the country's largest cities and metro areas are concentrated within the zero-elasticity category, which suggests that metro and city population size is a factor. However, the relationship of population size to segregation (racial and economic) is weak.

More significant is the "maturity" of the city. Table 2.12 depicts the average date by which cities in each group passed the 100,000 population mark. On the average the zero-elasticity cities passed the mark in 1881, the low-elasticity cities passed the mark in 1918, and the medium-elasticity cities passed the mark in 1933. As a group, high-elasticity cities reached the 100,000 inhabitant milestone only in 1953, the outset of the suburban era. The average hyper-elasticity city became a "big city" in 1960, well into the dominance of the suburban lifestyle.

A central city's age has many implications. By definition, an old city has an inventory of old, often decaying neighborhoods that typically become home to many poor people. A long-established Black or Hispanic population in an old city may have become highly isolated as victims of the social prejudices of an earlier era. Even an old city's long participation in certain social welfare programs, such as public housing, may reinforce racial and economic isolation. In any event, a city's age strongly influences racial and economic segregation within a metro area.

TABLE 2.12
INELASTIC CITIES ARE OLDER THAN ELASTIC CITIES

Area/City	Year when the population exceeded 100,000
Zero-Elasticity	1881
Low-Elasticity	1918
Medium-Elasticity	1933
High-Elasticity	1953
Hyper-Elasticity	1960

Finally, a central city's elasticity has the highest relationship of all these factors to the level of racial and economic segregation in a metro area. Why some central cities expanded and others did not must really be the subject of case-by-case studies. My five categories of elasticity bring together many different cities from many different regions, but some general observations can be made.

In general, state laws regarding annexation are less inhibiting in the South and West than they are in the Northeast and Midwest. Old cities (often in the Northeast and Midwest) had more neighbors to contend and compete with than had younger cities (often in the South and West).[12] The lesser ''racial gradients'' in the South and West raised fewer social and political barriers to a city's outward expansion. And being the hub of a more rapidly growing metro area created a more expansionist outlook among local public officials than was true of political leadership within more slowly expanding areas.

Finally, the relative unity or fragmentation of local government and institutions influences racial and economic segregation. Table 2.13 summarizes the rough picture in terms of local units of general government. The percentage of the area's population that is governed by the central city is listed in the first column. In effect, this statistic tells what proportion of the metro community falls under a single planning and zoning authority.

What does it mean for a zero-elasticity or low-elasticity city to have planning and zoning authority over 33 percent of the metro area population? It means little since that city is no longer

TABLE 2.13
FRAGMENTED LOCAL GOVERNMENT FOSTERS SEGREGATION;
UNIFIED LOCAL GOVERNMENT PROMOTES INTEGRATION

Area/City	Percentage of area population governed by central city	Number of suburban governments	Segregation index	
			Blacks	Hispanics
Zero-Elasticity	33%	120	0.72	0.57
Low-Elasticity	33	55	0.65	0.37
Medium-Elasticity	32	52	0.63	0.40
High-Elasticity	42	25	0.57	0.42
Hyper-Elasticity	44	23	0.57	0.37

planning for new growth that can capture a share of the middle-class, suburban-style population.

By contrast, it is significant when a high- or hyper-elasticity city represents 40 percent or more of the area because that city is planning for and capturing more than half of the area's suburban-style growth. How an elastic city government shapes the mix and distribution of new housing, new shopping areas, and new business parks makes a big difference in the future racial and economic profile of the area.

At first glance, the number of suburban governments in zero-elasticity metro areas is five-to-six times higher than in high- and hyper-elasticity metro areas. But after correcting for the larger population size of zero-elasticity areas, the fragmentation of suburban government drops to about a two-to-one ratio.

Nevertheless, the fragmentation of planning and zoning authority among multiple suburban governments in zero- and low-elasticity areas is serious because these suburban governments are planning for all of the area's new growth. Balkanization of the suburbs inevitably promotes exclusive planning and zoning. By contrast, the lesser balkanization of the suburbs around high- and hyper-elasticity cities is less significant because these independent, suburban governments are typically planning for less than half of the area's expansion.

The data in Table 2.13 must be treated with caution because they are a rough approximation of reality. What does an average of 120 suburban governments in zero-elasticity metro areas really mean? What are the planning and zoning powers of municipalities? Of townships? Of county governments? Must local governments zone in accordance with some areawide plan? The answers will vary from state to state.

In Table 2.13 I assume all units of local government have planning and zoning powers. That is certainly wrong. As a description of almost any specific metro area, that assumption is inaccurate.[13] As a characterization of an important factor shaping urban America, I believe that the observation is valid.

Table 2.14 relates the relative unity or fragmentation of public education to racial segregation in public school systems metrowide.

In some contrast to residential segregation, segregation of Black students in medium-, high-, and hyper-elasticity areas is much lower than it is in low- and zero-elasticity areas. This is because public education in many southern states is charac-

TABLE 2.14
DISPERSED AND FRAGMENTED PUBLIC EDUCATION IS MORE
SEGREGATED THAN CENTRALIZED AND UNIFIED PUBLIC EDUCATION

Metro Area	Percentage of metro area students enrolled in city schools	Number of suburban school districts*	School segregation index	
			Blacks	Hispanics
Zero-Elasticity	26%	45	0.71	0.59
Low-Elasticity	34	22	0.64	0.42
Medium-Elasticity	35	18	0.55	0.43
High-Elasticity	52	11	0.48	0.42
Hyper-Elasticity	49	12	0.47	0.38

*That maintain high schools.

terized by large countywide school systems that operate under long-standing racial integration plans. This has meant that southern schools are more integrated than southern neighborhoods. (Absent similar integration plans for Hispanic students, there is no such divergence between school segregation levels and neighborhood segregation levels for Hispanics.)

Do these differences in the degree of fragmentation of local government and local education help explain the differences in racial and economic segregation among different metro areas? I believe they do based both on my analysis and on personal experience as an elected public official. It matters whether a mayor or school board member shaping local policy sees poor Blacks, Hispanics, and Asians as "our people here" or "those people there." Too often suburban officials (and they are usually White) see "those people there," when they look at the declining, decaying, impoverished, minority-dominated inner city. Too often city officials (and they are increasingly Black and Hispanic) see "those people there" when they look at the still overwhelmingly White "outer city."

In a more unified area a mayor or school board member will see both groups as common constituents, (hopefully) as both deserving to be served in a fair and equitable way.

Lacking the precision with which the data support the first law of urban dynamics, I would argue that the evidence from all metro areas supports the second law of urban dynamics: fragmentation divides; unification unites.

Box 2.4 Complete Package Sells Albuquerque's Economy

As mayor of Albuquerque, I had many meetings with national corporations that were considering Albuquerque as a location for business expansion. What business was looking for was not cheap, nonunion labor. What business valued—and what we successfully sold them—was a total community package:

- an available labor force, reasonably prepared, very trainable, highly motivated, and with minimal racial and class antagonisms;
- a decent public school system (in Albuquerque's case, a metrowide system, whose operations are financed by state government, and whose capital construction is financed by a metrowide property tax levy);
- a respectable state university and a superb, business-oriented, technical-vocational institute (also funded by the state and by a metrowide tax levy);
- available, reasonably priced land, industrial bond financing (which almost all states now authorize), good transportation networks, and excellent energy supplies;
- a highly competent city government, adequately financed at moderate tax rates, with a tax base covering 80 percent of all residential property, and 90 percent of all commercial and industrial property in the metro area; and
- a livable, relaxed quality of life (although for some newcomers, New Mexico's high desert scenery and climate take getting used to).

These characteristics are by no means unique to Albuquerque. They typify the elastic communities I have been discussing.

And for Albuquerque they paid off in thousands of new jobs in high-tech manufacturing and regional and national business service centers.

What is the interaction between economic trends and these patterns of metro development? Table 2.15 outlines the growth of jobs in terms of city-suburb income ratios and rates of growth. As expected, job growth parallels the trends in population growth. The more elastic an area is, the higher its rate of job creation. As with overall population, the absolute increase in jobs created has been substantial in all groups.

Trends in manufacturing jobs (Table 2.16) reveal that deindustrialization has hit inelastic areas heavily. Between 1973 and

TABLE 2.15
ELASTIC AREAS HAVE FASTER RATES OF JOB CREATION
THAN INELASTIC AREAS

Metro Area	City/suburb per capita income rate, 1989	Metro job growth, 1973–88
Zero-Elasticity	71%	25%
Low-Elasticity	86	42
Medium-Elasticity	91	54
High-Elasticity	98	67
Hyper-Elasticity	104	71

1988 the zero-elasticity group lost 1.4 million manufacturing jobs (a 21-percent drop). All but five areas (Boston, Minneapolis–St. Paul, Oakland, Miami, and Washington, D.C.) lost manufacturing employment.

In industrial employment the low-elasticity group stagnated (1-percent gain). Manufacturing gains in Seattle and Tacoma, Washington; Norfolk–Newport News–Virginia Beach; Grand Rapids, Michigan; Atlanta and Savannah, Georgia; and Los Angeles offset losses elsewhere in this group.

The medium-elasticity group edged ahead in manufacturing jobs (8 percent) with Portland, Oregon; Lexington-Fayette, Kentucky; Ann Arbor, Michigan; Denver; Charlotte, North Carolina; Anaheim–Santa Ana, California; Oxnard-Ventura, California; Nashville; Wichita, Kansas; Madison; Macon, Georgia; Tulsa, Oklahoma; Tampa–St. Petersburg–Clearwater, Florida; and Knoxville, Tennessee showing gains.

TABLE 2.16
ELASTIC AREAS ADJUST BETTER TO ECONOMIC CHANGE THAN DO
INELASTIC AREAS

Metro Area	Percentage of metro manufacturing jobs		
	1973	1988	Growth 1973–88
Zero-Elasticity	18%	14%	−21%
Low-Elasticity	16	16	1
Medium-Elasticity	13	14	8
High-Elasticity	10	13	33
Hyper-Elasticity	8	11	35

Among the high- and hyper-elasticity groups manufacturing employment grew healthily (33 percent and 35 percent, respectively). Of the forty-three areas in these two groups, thirty-six experienced increases in manufacturing employment. Only in Memphis and Chattanooga, Tennessee; Baton Rouge, Louisiana; Columbus, Georgia; Beaumont–Port Arthur and Lubbock, Texas; and Little Rock, Arkansas did factory jobs decline (and generally the drop-off was slight).

Clearly, there is a regional pattern here. Is the deindustrialization of one part of the country and the modest industrialization of another part a simple Frostbelt-Sunbelt phenomenon? In part, yes. Most of the old, smokestack industries that have been driven out of business by international competition have been located in the Northeast or industrial Midwest. Jobs in certain industries (for example, steel and aluminum), once lost, are not recreated elsewhere in the country.

Urban areas, however, are not simply passive beneficiaries or victims of economic changes. Local areas can shape their futures. Detroit, for example, may have lost massive numbers of auto industry jobs, but other areas of the country have added automotive jobs (for example, Arlington, Texas, in the Dallas–Ft. Worth area; Smyrna, Tennessee, in the Nashville-Murfreesboro area; or Greenville-Spartanburg, South Carolina). An aging plant may be closed as obsolete, but its home region need not lose its replacement.[14] Moreover, an area can certainly nurture or compete for new businesses, based on new types of products and new types of services, which are the basis of most new "export product" jobs.

Each region has attractions in terms of the lifestyle it can offer. The Sunbelt does not have an inherent advantage over the Frostbelt. Many old cities, for example, have cultural facilities and institutions that are superior to those in newer cities. Climate and geography are matters of taste and adjustment. Inelastic areas are not without intrinsic competitive advantages.

What many inelastic areas have lost is the ability to compete. Business seeks out labor markets and economic regions, rarely specific governmental jurisdictions. Who speaks for greater Detroit or greater Cleveland, suffering from high political fragmentation, strong racial divisions, sharp income differentials, interjurisdictional competition—in short, from the loss of a shared sense of community and common destiny metrowide?

The economic data on the five categories of elasticity do show

TABLE 2.17
POVERTY IS MORE CONCENTRATED IN INELASTIC CITIES THAN IN
ELASTIC CITIES

Metro Area	Percentage of metro population below the poverty line, 1990	Percentage of city population below the poverty line, 1990	City's fair share index of metro area poor population, 1990
Zero-Elasticity	10%	21%	216%
Low-Elasticity	12	19	163
Medium-Elasticity	11	16	148
High-Elasticity	15	18	120
Hyper-Elasticity	13	15	115

regional biases. Most inelastic areas are in the Northeast and Midwest; most elastic areas are in the South and West. When examining rates of poverty metrowide (Table 2.17), we see that slightly higher percentages of the population of high-elasticity and hyper-elasticity areas fall under the poverty level than occurs in zero-elasticity and low-elasticity areas. One might conclude from this that the former group of communities is less effective at reducing poverty than the latter, but poverty levels have historically been higher in the South and West. In recent decades the rate of reduction of poverty has been greater in these regions as well (although somewhat slowed by the accelerating pace of immigration).

What is more critical for the health of central cities is that poverty is much more concentrated in inelastic cities than in elastic cities. Inelastic cities are cast in the role of home for most of their metro areas' poor minorities, as clearly indicated by disparities in the central cities' fair share of poverty index.

An even more complex picture is presented in Table 2.18, which shows the rate of growth in real per capita income metrowide over a twenty-year period. By my hypothesis, progress in real incomes should be least in zero-elasticity areas and greatest in hyper-elasticity areas. Instead, they are equal (39 percent).

Closer examination shows that average real income growth for the zero-elasticity group was buoyed by the powerful economic performances of America's flagship, postindustrial regions: New York, Boston, San Francisco, and Washington, D.C.

Box 2.5 Ties That Bind City and Suburbs

Two recent studies have examined the degree of interdependence of city and suburban economies.

Professor H. V. Savitch of the University of Louisville argues that "self-sufficiency neither was nor will be a modus operandi for cities and suburbs. As time goes by, interdependence, resource synergy and the ability to interact beyond exclusive spheres become important for metropolitan success. To do otherwise is to put suburbs at the edge of a sinkhole, whose slopes may be slippery."[1]

Savitch analyzed fifty-nine large metro areas. Those with central cities in the top income quartile generated over $2,000 more income per year per suburban resident than cities in the lowest quartile. Despite the impression of increasingly solitary suburbs, between 1979 and 1987 the interdependence became stronger. "A decade ago 47 percent of suburban income could be attributed to the density and income of the central city," Professor Savitch writes. "Today, that number has risen to 61 percent. Translated into earning capacity, for every $1,000 difference in city per capita income, suburbs stand to gain or lose $690."

Savitch also studied seven large central cities. The earnings generated by these cities rose in 1969–89, and the suburban share increased substantially in Baltimore, Denver, New Orleans, and Washington, D.C. Philadelphia's suburbanites increased their share of central city earnings modestly, while in St. Louis and

Almost sealed off from surrounding neighborhoods, the traditional downtowns continued as national and international centers of financial, information, government, and business services. Around the outlying beltways other information-age businesses blossomed. As metropolitan regions they maintained their national economic leadership.

For many, however, life within their cities deteriorated. Lacking necessary skills and ready transportation, many residents of inelastic cities did not benefit from downtown office jobs (skill barriers) or beltway-centered, high-tech manufacturing jobs (skill and transportation barriers). Gaps between income classes tended to grow wider within such regions.

From city hall's perspective, municipal bond ratings remain a key indicator of a city's long-term economic health (Table 2.19).

San Francisco suburbanites maintained their share of central city earnings. For all seven areas suburbanites accounted for between 34 percent (Philadelphia) and 63 percent (Washington, D.C.) of all earnings generated in central cities.

Savitch concluded that "whether cities are prosperous, what they do and how they do it matters. These conditions can mean the difference between metropolitan prosperity or decline. . . . Suburbs which surround healthy cities stand a better chance of vitality than those that surround sick cities. . . . Self-sufficiency at the periphery is not a sufficient defense. The challenge of repair is as much for those outside the center as for those in it."

In a study of 28 metro areas in the Northeast and Middle West, Richard Voith, a senior economist for the Federal Reserve Bank of Philadelphia, also found high correlations in growth of real incomes and employment between central city and suburban economies. He concluded that "decline in central cities is likely to be associated with slow-growing suburbs. Even if the most acute problems associated with urban decline do not arise in the suburbs, central city decline is likely to be a long-run, slow drain on the economic and social vitality of the region."[2]

1. H. V. Savitch, "Ties That Bind: Central Cities, Suburbs and the New Metropolitan Region" (unpublished).
2. Richard Voith, "City and Suburban Growth: Substitutes or Complements?", in the *Business Review* of the Federal Reserve Bank of Philadelphia, September–October 1992, p. 31.

Although zero-elasticity cities are in the wealthiest metro areas, they have bond ratings that are lower than their municipal counterparts in other categories. Medium-elasticity cities have the highest bond ratings; in general their economies are more fully developed and mature than are the economies of areas that are growing more spectacularly.

The Point of No Return

Table 2.20 focuses on those cities that have passed the "point of no return" that I defined in Chapter I. A dozen cities had dropped economically to the level where city incomes were only about 70 percent of suburban income. At this point city-suburb

TABLE 2.18
METRO INCOME GROWTH IN ELASTIC AND INELASTIC AREAS
HAS BEEN EQUAL

Metro Area	Percentage growth in real per capita income metrowide, 1969–89
Zero-Elasticity	39%
Low-Elasticity	32
Medium-Elasticity	38
High-Elasticity	38
Hyper-Elasticity	39

economic disparities become so severe that the city, in a broad sense, no longer is a place to invest or create jobs (except in some fortress-type downtowns). All twelve cities lost more economic ground to their suburbs, with Gary, Detroit, Cleveland, Trenton, and Hartford seeing the gap with their suburbs widening at catastrophic rates. Overall, these twelve cities' income levels dropped from 63 percent to 55 percent of suburban levels.

The minority percentages of all twelve cities also climbed rapidly (from 58 to 63 percent). The increase was more a function of the continuing exodus of Whites (along with middle-class Blacks and Hispanics) rather than of increasing numbers of minority poor.

Finally, the overall populations of nine of the twelve continued to drop with only New Haven, Hartford, and Paterson halting their decline (at least during the 1980s—all because of Hispanic immigration).

TABLE 2.19
ELASTIC CITIES HAVE BETTER BOND RATINGS THAN DO
INELASTIC CITIES

City	City bond rating*
Zero-Elasticity	5.52
Low-Elasticity	6.59
Medium-Elasticity	7.98
High-Elasticity	7.18
Hyper-Elasticity	7.14

*Numerical values assigned to Moody's bond ratings are AAA=10.0; AA=8.0; A=6.0; BAA=4.0; BA=2.0; and B=1.0.

TABLE 2.20

IN INELASTIC CITIES PAST THE POINT OF NO RETURN, THE POPULATION CONTINUES TO DECLINE, THE MINORITY RATIO CONTINUES TO INCREASE, AND THE CITY-SUBURB INCOME GAP CONTINUES TO WIDEN

City	Change in city population*		Percentage of minorities in city		City-suburb income ratio	
	By 1980	By 1990	1980	1990	1979	1989
Chicago, Ill.	-17%	-23%	57%	60%	69%	66%
New Haven, Conn.	-23	-21	44	47	70	62
Philadelphia, Pa.	-19	-23	42	45	72	64
Gary, Ind.	-15	-25	81	85	71	59
Detroit, Mich.	-35	-44	69	77	67	53
Baltimore, Md.	-17	-23	57	60	68	64
Cleveland, Ohio	-37	-45	48	50	63	54
Trenton, N.J.	-28	-31	54	59	66	50
Hartford, Conn.	-23	-21	61	66	63	53
Paterson, N.J.	-1	-3	64	72	52	47
Bridgeport, Conn.	-10	-11	46	50	49	41
Newark, N.J.	-25	-38	77	82	48	42

*Population changes are measured from the city's peak population.

Box 2.6 Research Documents Black Ghetto Expansion

In a study of 318 metro areas between 1980 and 1990, Paul Jargowsky, a University of Texas at Dallas social scientist, has found that Black ghetto poverty has increased significantly.[1]

Defining a Black ghetto as an urban census tract in which 40 percent or more of the Black population is poor (in 1989, an income of less than $10,360 for a family of three), Jargowsky found that the number of Blacks living in ghetto areas increased 36 percent from 4.3 million to 5.9 million.

The percentage of the total Black population living in ghetto areas increased from 20 percent to almost 24 percent—which, however, means that over three-quarters of the Black population does not live in urban ghettos.

On the other hand, poor Blacks are increasingly isolated from the Black middle class in urban ghettos. The proportion of poor urban Blacks in ghetto areas increased from 37 percent to 45 percent while, on the average, poor households edged past the fifty percent level in such areas for the first time.

Most ominous for many city officials, the physical size of urban ghettos expanded dramatically during the 1980s even as, with the flight of the Black middle class to suburbs, the population density of ghettos declined. The number of census tracts classified as ghettos grew from 3,256 to 5,003—a 54 percent increase!—while population density declined −11 percent in ghetto areas.

"From the point of view of local political officials, the increase in the size of the ghetto is a disaster," Jargowsky comments. "Many of those leaving the ghetto settle in nonghetto areas outside the political jurisdiction of the central city. Thus, the geographic size of the ghetto is expanding, cutting a wider swath through the hearts of our metropolitan areas."

This shows the fourth law of urban dynamics at work: ghettos only become bigger ghettos.

Cities without Suburbs

The cities in Table 2.20 are doing very poorly even though they are located in some of the country's wealthiest areas. This section examines the other extreme—cities that are doing well even

Jargowsky finds that ghetto poverty is a function of both racial segregation and metropolitan economic growth. During the 1980s, the proportion of Blacks living in ghettos increased most dramatically in the declining industrial states and oil patch communities caught in the oil and real estate slump. By contrast, booming, postindustrial economies around Boston, Hartford, New York, Philadelphia, Baltimore, and Washington allowed many middle-class Blacks to leave ghettos for new suburban homes.

"Ghetto poverty," Jargowsky concludes, "is not primarily the product of a 'ghetto culture' that discourages upward mobility, but the product of metropolitan labor markets and residential settlement patterns. Ghetto self-help programs, enterprise zones, etc., cannot alter the fundamental dynamics of metropolitan economies or the evolving geography of residential location decisions.

"Vigorous enforcement of antidiscrimination in housing, scatter-site public housing, and zoning requirements that encourage mixed-income developments can all play a role in reducing the segregation of Blacks and the Black poor," Jargowsky recommends. "This has both an immediate effect—reducing ghetto poverty—and an indirect, long-term effect—the increased earnings potential of children who attend better schools, grow up in safer, more stimulating environments, and see better role models of success in the mainstream economy."

1. Paul A. Jargowsky, "Ghetto Poverty among Blacks in the 1980s," (January 15, 1993; unpublished paper). The *U.S. News and World Report* reported Jargowsky's findings in an article entitled "The Shifting State of Black Ghettos" (January 18, 1993).

though they are located in modest-income metro areas. These are all cities that dominate their areas. They are, in effect, cities without suburbs (see Table 2.21).

I have applied two standards to identify a city without suburbs. First, the city must house 50 percent or more of the metro population. On this basis, for example, prominent cities like San Diego and Houston miss the cut. Second, the average per capita income of city residents must be 90 percent or more of the average per capita income of suburban residents. Below this stan-

TABLE 2.21
Twenty-three Cities without Suburbs

Metro Area	Percentage of metro area residents living in city, 1990	City-suburb income ratio, 1989	Per capita income of metro residents, 1989	Change in per capita income, 1967–87	Residential segregation index for Blacks	1991 city bond rating*
Jackson, Miss.	50%	99%	$12,311	44%	0.67	6.00
Nashville-Davidson, Tenn.	50	98	14,567	49	0.61	10.00
Madison, Wis.	52	95	15,542	34	0.48	10.00
Tulsa, Okla.	52	129	13,783	32	0.62	8.00
Reno, Nev.	53	97	16,365	26	0.37	5.50
Fresno, Calif.	53	95	11,824	27	0.52	5.50
Tallahassee, Fla.	53	102	13,122	37	0.52	6.00
Omaha, Nebr.-Iowa	54	95	13,989	31	0.70	10.00
Shreveport, La.	59	103	11,530	37	0.60	6.00
Indianapolis-Marion, Ind.	59	90	15,159	32	0.74	10.00
Austin, Tex.	60	96	14,521	51	0.56	6.00

Wichita, Kans.	63	104	14,303	52	0.64	8.00
Montgomery, Ala.	64	112	12,258	44	0.60	6.00
Lexington-Fayette, Ky.	65	124	13,945	41	0.54	6.00
Huntsville, Ala.	67	117	15,443	46	0.57	8.00
Jacksonville-Duval, Fla.	70	90	14,141	50	0.58	6.00
Colorado Springs, Colo.	71	116	13,664	39	0.44	8.50
Corpus Christi, Tex.	74	129	11,065	34	0.56	5.50
Columbus-Muskogee, Ga.-Ala.	74	127	11,282	34	0.58	6.00
Albuquerque, N. Mex.	80	118	13,594	41	0.39	8.00
Lubbock, Tex.	84	118	12,008	31	0.60	8.00
Lincoln, Nebr.	90	94	13,803	30	0.43	8.00
Anchorage, Alaska	100	100	19,620	39	0.35	6.00
23 Cities without Suburbs-Means	65	111	$13,819	38	0.55	7.26
94 Other Metro Area-Means	31%	87%	$15,131	34%	0.65	6.63*

*Numerical values assigned to Moody's bond ratings are AAA=10.0; AA=8.0; A=6.0; BAA=4.0; BA=2.0; and B=1.0.

dard continual suburbanization of the middle class is occurring. San Antonio, San Jose, and Tucson represent 70 percent or more of their metro populations; however, average incomes within the three cities have fallen to about 72 percent of suburban levels. This widening income gap excludes them from the table and suggests significant future problems for all three cities.

Twenty-three cities meet my cities-without-suburbs criteria. Five are consolidated governments: Nashville-Davidson; Indianapolis-Marion; Lexington-Fayette, Kentucky; Jackson-ville-Duval, Florida; and Columbus-Muskogee, Georgia. The others have maintained their dominance of the local area through aggressive annexation policies.

None of these communities is Paradise. None are exempt from the social problems of modern-day America. Two cities without suburbs—Corpus Christi, Texas, and Columbus, Geor-gia—are located in regions that are particularly poor economi-cally. Others are in areas of modest incomes. Only Madison, Reno, Indianapolis, Huntsville, and Anchorage break through the $15,000 average income threshold. The average per capita income in the 23 metro areas is $13,819—$1,300 below the aver-age for the other 94 metro areas in our sample of 117 areas. Yet these cities and their residents are doing pretty well.

City without suburb incomes are 106 percent of suburban in-comes. City levels fall to 85 percent of suburban levels in the other ninety-four metro areas. Average city incomes in the twenty-three cities without suburbs ($14,012) are solidly higher than average city incomes in the remaining ninety-four cities ($13,320).

That advantage is gradually widening. Over a twenty-year period (1969–89), real per capita incomes in the metro areas of the cities without suburbs increased 38 percent compared with a 34-percent increase in the other ninety-four metro areas. As metro regions, cities without suburbs are gradually catching up with the rest of the country while maintaining superior real income standards for their city residents.

Although their metro economies are still modest, cities with-out suburbs have better bond ratings (7.26 compared with 6.63) than the rest of the sample has. None of the twenty-three has less than an A (5.5) bond rating. And of great significance, the level of racial segregation is lower—0.55 compared with 0.65—yet still far from an acceptable level.

In summary, cities without suburbs are making the most of

modest economic circumstances. What would happen if inelastic cities began to tap the resources and opportunities of genuinely wealthy areas? Chapter III will discuss some of the possibilities.

Notes

1. These smaller metro areas are "free-standing" areas, not outlying regions of larger metropolitan areas, except Racine, Wisconsin (part of the greater Milwaukee area), and Vineland-Millville-Bridgeton, New Jersey (part of the greater Philadelphia area). Except for many metro areas located in Florida, Texas, and California, these smaller metro areas are relatively slow-growing urban nodes, small manufacturing communities, or commercial centers for agricultural and natural resource regions. In 1950 only 9 out of the 131 areas (Amarillo and Waco, Texas; Asheville, North Carolina; Cedar Rapids, Iowa; Decatur and Springfield, Illinois; Pueblo, Colorado; St. Joseph, Missouri; and Topeka, Kansas) were considered important enough by the Census Bureau to rank as Metropolitan Areas. Most of the nine have quietly—and perhaps not unhappily—watched the world pass them by.

2. Charleston, West Virginia, is an exception. Its vigorous economic prosperity is largely the result of Charleston's having developed a replacement resource for coal—U.S. Senator Robert Byrd's influence in directing federal spending to projects in his state.

3. Of course, "White-only metro areas" are not discrimination-free communities. Interestingly, however, none of these metro areas has developed a significant income gap between the central city and the suburbs. The city-suburb income ratios range between 94 percent (Manchester-Nashua, New Hampshire) and 119 percent (Boise, Idaho). Through annexation their central cities (omitting New England) have expanded vigorously in area (153 percent) and moderately in population (63 percent). The very absence of city-suburb income gaps and elasticity-limiting conditions suggests the role that racial issues play as drivers of urban growth patterns and city-suburb disparities in many other metro areas.

4. Although these categories represent groupings by decile, they contain uneven numbers of metro areas (for example, thirty zero-elastic areas and nineteen low-elastic areas.) The reason is that the elasticity scores were calculated for all 522 central cities, split into three different sizes. The apparent unevenness of the categories results from my decision to deal with only one central city in a metro area. For example, Scottsdale, Tempe, and Mesa, Arizona, are all hyper-elastic central cities in the Phoenix metro area, but they are not added to the hyper-elastic category because Phoenix is the only central city treated in my analysis for that metro area.

5. The Pittsburgh, New York, Jersey City, and St. Joseph, Missouri, areas were the only metro areas, except for the "Declining mining regions," actually to lose population (-8, -1, -15 and -14 percent, respectively). The New York–northern New Jersey–Connecticut CMSA gained 4 million people, or 29 percent.

6. These cities were New Orleans; Akron and Dayton, Ohio; Erie and Allentown, Pennsylvania; and Flint, Michigan.

7. The exceptions are Los Angeles; Columbus, Ohio; Honolulu, Hawaii; and Tacoma, Washington.

8. These were Richmond, Virginia; Gary and South Bend, Indiana; Birmingham, Alabama; and Kansas City, Missouri.

9. These were Lansing, Michigan; Rockford, Illinois; Denver, Colorado; Omaha, Nebraska; Indianapolis; Des Moines, Iowa; Macon, Georgia; and Knoxville, Tennessee.

10. Cities that may be past their peak are Memphis and Chattanooga, Tennessee; Fort Lauderdale, Florida; Shreveport, Louisiana; Beaumont, Texas; Mobile, Alabama; Jackson, Mississippi; and Little Rock, Arkansas. All except Chattanooga are down 6 percent or less from recent population peaks.

11. Of necessity, as in Chapter I, I have used school segregation indices for Hispanics where residential segregation indices have not been calculated by the census bureau.

12. Having already been surrounded by smaller municipalities is the largest single factor preventing further expansion by the oldest, zero-elastic "giants" of the Northeast and Midwest. That does not explain the relative inelasticity of many older cities other than New York, Chicago, Detroit, Philadelphia, and Boston. Moreover, racial and political motives to "contain" the old cities often played a role in the founding of old suburbs as well.

13. Consider the example of Albuquerque. My data show that the Albuquerque area has a central city covering 80 percent of the population, with three suburban governments covering the remaining 20 percent. In reality, two of the three suburban governments are tiny municipalities that account for less than 3 percent of the metro area's population. There are only two planning and zoning authorities of consequence: the city of Albuquerque and Bernalillo County. For years Bernalillo County contracted with the city for professional planning services. Both adopted a common Comprehensive Growth Plan. In the case of a serious dispute, the city can invoke extraterritorial planning and zoning powers within five miles of its city limits.

In short, each metro area has its own story to tell, which is why my statistical characterization is true in the large, but never wholly accurate in the small.

14. The city of Detroit has recently succeeded in getting automakers to build two new plants for six thousand workers but is losing headquarters jobs to its suburbs.

Chapter III

Strategies for Stretching Cities

Reversing the fragmentation of urban areas is an essential step in ending severe racial and economic segregation. The "city" must be redefined to reunify city and suburb. Ideally, such re-unification is achieved through metropolitan government.

Three Strategies

Having a metropolitan government is much better than trying to get multiple local governments to act like a metropolitan government. The former is a more lasting and stable framework for sustained, long-term action.

The practical benefits of unification, however, can be achieved if local governments follow (or have imposed on them) three strategies: end fiscal imbalance through revenue sharing between rich and poor jurisdictions; diminish racial and economic segregation through affordable housing requirements and housing assistance programs metrowide; and, finally, promote metrowide economic development.

Revenue sharing alone is inadequate; no amount of money can salvage isolated inner cities. Areawide housing programs are slow to take hold and most effective within a vigorously growing economy. A beltway-centered and downtown-centered economic boom does not trickle down to inner city ghettos and barrios. All three strategies are inseparable and indispensable parts of a successful approach.

End Fiscal Imbalance

By taxing a larger share of the wealth of metro areas, a metro government matches resources to problems. Metropolitaniza-

85

tion eliminates local fiscal imbalances under which inner cities, grappling with the lion's share of social problems, face dwindling tax resources.

From the perspective of fiscal equalization, the case for metro government is quite clear. The benefits would flow automatically from metropolitanization.

DIMINISH RACIAL AND ECONOMIC SEGREGATION

Through planning and zoning powers and government housing assistance plans, a local government can help shape where different economic classes live. A broad-based government is not generally as afflicted with the "Not-in-My-Backyard" syndrome as is a narrow-based government. A broad-based government can carry out zoning policies and capital outlay plans that encourage the private market to bring more mixed-income neighborhoods into being. Within its wide jurisdiction a broad-based government is able to scatter public housing projects and implement rent subsidy programs across a variety of neighborhoods. It is, in effect, able to follow strategies of dispersion of low-income groups, if it chooses, and, through dispersion, to reduce the very severity and incidence of social stress.

That a metro government would pursue automatically such policies is not guaranteed. What is clear, however, is that a highly fragmented metro area has little ability to agree on socially controversial policies, absent powerful compulsion by state or federal law.

PROMOTE AREAWIDE ECONOMIC PROGRESS

Metro areas with a dominant government have a more cohesive community spirit. More effective public-private coalitions form to promote common interests. Internecine warfare among local jurisdictions is minimized. Such genuine communities are able to compete on the terms the marketplace most values—namely, as integrated, total labor market areas.

Is advocating metro government a feasible strategy? Successfully challenging racial and class attitudes undergirding the fragmentation of many urban areas is the toughest political task in America. To that daunting challenge must be added overcoming the stolid inertia of the status quo. In fact, widespread skepticism among the "experts" may be the greatest initial barrier to implementing my proposals. The slow progress of voluntary regional cooperation and the few successful efforts at forming metro governments have made many planners skeptical about reform. Who can seriously advocate metro government for New York, Chicago, Philadelphia, or Detroit, for example?

My proposals should not be judged by how immediately feasible they might be for the hardest cases. The United States of America is a big and varied country. There are 316 other metro areas besides New York, Chicago, Philadelphia, and Detroit. Most metro areas would benefit substantially from metropolitan approaches.

Urban "Triage"

In effect, a national urban policy should recognize metropolitanization as a type of urban "triage." The different stages might be called preventive medicine, out-patient treatment, major surgery, and life-support systems.

Preventive medicine would apply to most small metropolitan areas (fewer than 200,000 residents) where an urban core exists within a rural or semirural region. The most effective preventive medicine would be to merge immediately the core city and the surrounding county into a unified government. (Over 90 percent of the small metro areas are single-county areas.)

Unifying city and county governments is not essential as long as the core city exercises broad annexation powers over urbanizing areas (including areas in adjacent counties). In addition, a core city should have the power to veto the incorporation of any competing new municipalities within a certain distance of its city limits.

In effect, preventive medicine inoculates against the emergence of fiscal disparities. It also tends to immunize a youthful metro area against the development of sharp jurisdictional schisms along racial and class lines.

Like all preventive medicine, inoculation and immunization would be relatively cheap. State legislatures must ensure that the right laws are on the books. Such laws should cover municipal annexation powers, conditions for municipal incorporation, and consolidation of local governments.

Most of the high- and hyper-elasticity metro areas that are large should receive *out-patient treatment*. By no means are they ill now, but as they grow out of adolescence, they will become less resistant to the ills that come with maturity.

Maintaining the ability of high- and hyper-elasticity cities to grow through annexation is important. Increasingly, however, they are surrounded by independent suburbs that, like parasites, draw off their hosts' vigor. Parasitism can be combated through city-county consolidation. City-county consolidation is tough political medicine, but it can be self-administered locally, given the right prescription.

Low- and medium-elasticity areas are subtly infected with a still operable cancer: incipient central city decline amid suburban growth. Left untreated, the city-suburb schism will become fatal. The cancer, however, is so imbedded that it cannot be excised by purely local action. *Major surgery* is required by state government in the form of city-county consolidation or state mandates regarding areawide revenue sharing and areawide affordable housing strategies. The path to a complete cure is long and arduous, but a cure is achievable if the patient is in the hands of skilled professionals. Purely home remedies will not cure the ills of low- and medium-elasticity areas.

Zero-elasticity areas are candidates for *life-support systems*. Their disease is so far advanced that, for many, there is no long-term cure in any organic sense. Many of these cities are in highly complex, multicounty (or even multistate) metropolitan regions. Single-county consolidation would not have a dramatic impact on such a city's health, although it would be better than no action whatsoever. Yet forging multicounty metropolitan government would be extraordinarily difficult.

Life-support systems emphasize limited-in-scope policies that have some of the benefits of metro government, but do not require actual governmental reorganization. Such actions would include major state and federal urban aid programs targeted on cities suffering major fiscal disparities; state or federal guarantees of central city bonds to reduce financing costs; state or county assumption of financing (and administering) certain central city programs; state-mandated, areawide affordable housing compacts, and so on.

Life-support systems are designed to keep zero-elasticity cities alive. They cannot make them well. For some zero-elasticity cities a miracle could happen—a political conversion that would clear away the seemingly insurmountable political barriers to drastic reform. Absent such a miracle, many zero-elasticity cities may die. With their death, their suburbs may wither away as well. Limbs cannot survive without the heart.

Metro Government: A Definition

Before examining the mechanisms and politics of creating metro governments, I need to offer a working definition of what a metro government is. The country abounds with 28,078 special purpose units of local government (transit authorities, water and sewer agencies, and community college districts, for example). Often they are metrowide. Although creating special purpose governments can be an effective strategy toward ultimately achieving metropolitan unification, a true metro government must be a general purpose local government. It must have all of the powers of a municipality under applicable state law. Moreover, it must exercise exclusive powers within its jurisdiction. In other words, it must not be a general government that fills in the interstices between on-going major municipal enclaves. This, unfortunately, is the situation of many county governments in urban areas.

A metro government need not be responsible for all local public functions. Depending on local conditions, special purpose governments can still exist, but a metro government must control key planning and zoning powers. These decisions must not be subject to veto by other local bodies.

Although a metro government need not cover the entire metro area, it should contain at least 60 percent of the area's population. Moreover, a metro government must contain the region's central city (or a preponderance of multiple central cities).

I have categorized metro governments in three classes based on the percentage of the metro area population that is served. Class III serves between 60 percent and 74 percent of the metro population. Class II serves between 75 percent and 99 percent of the metro population. Class I serves 100 percent of the metro population.[1]

State Government Initiatives

Although this book is written from Washington, D.C., it is based on my experiences as a mayor and state legislator. Restructuring local governance is not primarily a task for the federal government. It is primarily the responsibility of citizens and political leaders at the local and state levels.

As I stated earlier, successfully challenging racial and class attitudes underlying the fragmentation of many metro areas is the toughest political task in America. Rarely will a White county commissioner or Black mayor both champion actions to unify metro areas (in more than a limited and voluntary way) *and* survive local voter backlash (White and Black alike).

America, however, is a *federal* system. Within the bounds of our national constitution, the states have sovereign powers. To varying degrees, local governments (and local school districts) are legal subjects of state government. State legislatures frame the standards and procedures by which new municipalities are created. Typically, state governments do more than merely set the ground rules for local initiative. Most state legislatures can also create new local governments and merge old ones (including school districts)—often without a constitutional requirement for local voter approval.

Furthermore, governors and state legislators can and do act as metrowide policymakers. There are instances when state governments have mandated areawide local cooperation in a wide range of functional activities (transportation planning, sewage treatment, air quality control, senior citizens programs) or—much more rarely—areawide tax sharing or areawide affordable housing programs.

State government also plays an increasingly important role in revenue sharing for local government and, above all, for local school systems. By 1990 state aid had grown to 17 percent of city government revenues and 36 percent of county government revenues. State responsibility for funding local school districts had grown by 1988 to 39 percent. With the purse comes additional power (and responsibility) to provide for the more rational and equitable organization of metro areas.

Statutory authority aside, however, why should state legislators and governors have any greater political opportunity to implement unpopular reforms? Are they not elected by the same voters as local officials?

The obvious answer is "yes, but not all." Although the metro proportion continues to grow, in 1990 almost one-quarter of the nation's population (22 percent) still lived outside metro areas. About one-third (35 percent) lived in central cities. At least hypothetically, there is a legislative majority embodied in a city-rural alliance against suburban resistance. Admittedly, in most states this is an improbable alliance now, given the lack of perceived common cause.

UNIFY LOCAL GOVERNMENTS

There are three different ways metropolitan governments can be created. In single-county metro areas, urban county governments can be fully empowered and municipal governments abolished; or county and municipal governments can be consolidated into new, unified governments. In multicounty metro areas, cities and existing counties can be combined into a single, regional government. Each of these three options will be discussed in turn.

Empowering urban counties.   Except in New England, counties have been the basic framework of local government within which municipalities (a more intensive form of local government) come into being. Counties typically predate urban development. They are the creation of a state or territorial legislature, which initially partitioned the state or territory's land into large governing units. County jurisdictions are remarkably stable. There are today 3,042 counties in the United States; forty years ago there were 3,052 counties. (Such stability has given rise to the adage that "the legislature may create municipalities, but only God can create a county.")

County government has been the government of rural and small-town America. As urbanization occurs, municipalities are formed to control development through planning and zoning and to provide a more intensive level of local services. Generally, county government continues to be responsible countywide (including within municipalities) for certain services—the county courts (state criminal trials), county assessor (property tax assessment), county treasurer (property tax collection), county clerk (records and elections), and often a county hospital (indigent health care). In addition, counties provide public services (roads, parks, fire and police protection) to unincorporated areas of the county.

Over the decades, however, as areas have urbanized around older cities, counties have been empowered by legislatures to provide full municipal-type services to unincorporated areas. Urban county governments often rival or exceed major city governments in size and scope. Moreover, although county government is often more limited in the array of taxes it can levy, its tax base is much broader than that of municipal governments within its boundaries. (County government bond ratings are typically one full level above bond ratings of inelastic central cities located within them.)

County government, when developed to the greatest extent, becomes a major deliverer of urban services, such as the government of Los Angeles County. County government may become the dominant local unit of government, both providing services and controlling area development. Montgomery County, Maryland, is an outstanding example (see Box 2.3).

The most direct—and probably most efficient—path to creating metropolitan government in the majority of metro areas is to empower urban county government, have it absorb the functions and responsibilities of all municipal governments within its boundaries, and abolish all municipalities. This is an action that is fully within the legal powers of most state legislatures even if at present such sweeping urban reorganization is beyond legislators' desires and political powers.

Consolidating cities and counties.   Typically, movements to create areawide governmental units have focused on consolidating municipal governments with their surrounding county governments. In recent decades the most notable consolidations have merged the central city with single counties. Indianapolis-Marion County, Nashville-Davidson County, Jacksonville-Duval County are examples. (On the Indianapolis-Marion County consolidation, see Box 3.1; on the Nashville-Davidson County consolidation, see Box. 3.2.)

Each city-county consolidation has been custom-made for its area. The ultimate structure represents a compromise with tradition and political realities. Traditional functions of county government may be absorbed into the new, unified government (Nashville-Davidson) or continued as independent functions

Box 3.1 Unigov Propels Indianapolis to Big League Status

On a wintry midnight in January 1983, big vans moved the NFL's Baltimore Colts to Indianapolis. This dark night will live in infamy for Baltimore civic boosters, but it announced to the world that Indianapolis had arrived in "the bigs."

The crucial step toward acquiring a pro football team was probably taken on January 1, 1970, when "Unigov" came into existence. The consolidation of the city of Indianapolis and Marion County by legislative act was the first to occur without a popular referendum since New York City was created in 1898.

The legislature's action originated with the Greater Indianapolis Progress Committee's Task Force on Government Structure. Appointed in 1968 by Richard Lugar (then mayor, now U.S. senator), the task force of civic, business, and government leaders drafted an eighty-six-page bill modeled in part on the Jacksonville and Nashville consolidations. The task force then lobbied it through the legislature.

"Unigov" was something of a misnomer. Three small municipalities, sixteen townships, and separate hospital and airport authorities were left unconsolidated. A dozen county constitutional offices were continued, including the office of the Marion County sheriff. Public education was left in twenty-two separate school districts, bolstering more racial segregation than characterizes other consolidated communities. (Indeed, many in Indianapolis's Black community felt Unigov was designed to dilute the emerging voting power of Blacks.)

Consolidation, however, instantly re-energized Indianapolis, expanding its tax base and cementing a blue-chip municipal bond rating. Lugar's successor as mayor, William Hudnut, praises Unigov. "It brought better delivery of services and lower taxes— taxes that don't go up as fast. Equally important, consolidation has created a wider sense of community that helps you sell your city."[1] Selling their city, Unigov and the business community set out to promote Indianapolis into becoming a major, year-round sports venue.

New Year's Day, 1970. Baltimore should have "heard footsteps."

1. "Group Hears Indianapolis Mayor Laud Consolidation," *Albuquerque Journal*, March 2, 1991.

Box 3.2 Consolidation Played Right Tune for Music City, USA

By 1960 the city of Nashville's population was dropping, its downtown decaying, and many leading businesses were preparing to leave. Thirty years later Nashville-Davidson is the booming heart of a million-person region, the music industry capital of the country, and Tennessee's undisputed center of government, insurance, banking, and apparel manufacturing.

The turning point was the consolidation of Nashville with surrounding Davidson County—an action approved by the voters in 1962 although they had rejected another consolidation proposal four years earlier. In one step a city of 73 square miles and 170,000 people became a city of 473 square miles and 399,000 people. (Today Nashville has a population of 488,000.)

Beverly Briley, then county executive of Davidson County, led the successful campaign for consolidation over the opposition of Nashville's mayor and many entrenched city councillors. A decade later Mayor Briley had high praise for the new Metro. "Prior to consolidation, the business community was fed up. I believe there is a direct relation between Metro and the revitalization that downtown Nashville is experiencing."[1]

Metro brought about a complete consolidation of all municipal and county functions. "County" residents' fears of higher taxes were assuaged by charter provisions for two services districts: an urban services district (the old city) with higher services and higher taxes, and a general services district (countywide). Areas formerly in the county petitioned to be "annexed" into the urban services district.

1. Quoted in "Nashville Thrives on a County-City Merger," *Business Week* (September 25, 1971): 133.

while the new government assumes service-providing functions for all unincorporated areas (Indianapolis-Marion County). Bowing to political reality, certain municipal enclaves may remain (for example, the town of Speedway within Indianapolis), and rural residents may have to be reassured through creation of lower service, lower tax zones (Nashville).

Despite such compromises, city-county consolidations do initially achieve the key goals: unification of the tax base and centralization of planning and zoning authority. With the continued spread of suburbia and long-distance commuting, the long-term dilemma is that metro areas often grow beyond the consolidated boundaries of the consolidated governments. Indianapolis–Marion County, Nashville–Davidson County, and Jacksonville–Duval County were all highly successful consolidations of the 1960s. Today Indianapolis–Marion County is 59 percent of its ten-county metro area; Nashville–Davidson, 50 percent of its six-county area; and Jacksonville-Duval County, 70 percent of its five-county area. With the populations of outlying counties growing rapidly, their metropolitanization must be updated.

Combining counties into regional governments.   The most significant multicounty combination is also the least remembered: the creation of New York City in 1898 (Box 1.2). Several independent local communities in what are now New York City's five boroughs were combined. For its first fifty years the consolidated result—New York City—functioned very well. Since the 1950s, however, the consequences of the White middle-class movement to the suburbs and the burgeoning low-income Black and Hispanic populations within the city have largely obscured New York City's earlier success as a consolidated, multicounty regional government.

CONSOLIDATION IMPACT

By whatever method achieved state by state, recasting urban government on a unified, single-county basis would create metropolitan governments in most urban areas. Today only 48 of 320 metropolitan areas are served by metro governments as I have defined them (see Table 3.1).

Most are medium-size communities. Of the forty-eight— which are scattered among twenty-one states—the largest are

TABLE 3.1
CURRENT METRO GOVERNMENTS

Class of metro government	Number of metro areas	Population	Percentage of national population
III	32	5,818,158	2.3%
II	15	2,311,829	0.9
I	1	226,330	0.1
Totals	48	8,356,317	3.3

TABLE 3.2
POTENTIAL METRO GOVERNMENTS AFTER
SINGLE-COUNTY UNIFICATION

Class of metro government	Number of metro areas	Population	Percentage of national population
III	51	22,916,117	9.2%
II	46	24,381,322	9.8
I	158	57,057,701	23.0
Totals	256	104,355,140	42.0

San Antonio (935,933), Jacksonville (635,230), Memphis (610,337), El Paso (513,342), Tucson (405,390), and Albuquerque (384,736).

Fully empowering urban county government or consolidating central cities with home counties would revolutionize urban governance for most of the nation. As Table 3.2 shows, 256 metro areas could be served by metro government.

Sixty metro areas (including twenty-one of the forty-six metro areas of 1,000,000 or more residents) would not reach the minimum threshold for a metro government (that is, 60 percent) by single-county unification. New York, Philadelphia, Detroit, Washington, D.C., Boston, and Atlanta are in this category. More far-reaching measures would be needed for these areas to achieve greater metropolitan unity.

Conversely, many of the nation's biggest metro areas—among them, Chicago, Cleveland, Pittsburgh, Milwaukee, Buffalo, and Oakland—would be substantially unified. Included are zero-elasticity areas suffering from inner-city isolation as well as more elastic areas.

Even more significant, however, countywide unification would metropolitanize most of the country's medium-size and smaller urban areas. Table 3.3 summarizes the effect by metro population size. For the remainder, achieving metropolitan government would require multicounty combinations.

City-county consolidation has been relatively rare—only nineteen since World War II. In fact, only sixteen states have specific statutes authorizing city-county consolidation and setting forth the procedures for its achievement (see Table 3.4). Of the sixteen states, seven are in the West, five in the South, four in the Midwest, and none in the Northeast, where counties hardly exist as meaningful governmental units. Except for Colorado,

TABLE 3.3
POTENTIAL UNIFICATION IMPACT AFTER
SINGLE-COUNTY UNIFICATION

Metro population	Number of metro areas	Number of metro governments	Percentage of metro areas with metro government
1.0 Million+	46	25	54%
.500–.999	46	37	80
.200–.499	93	79	85
.050–.199	130	119	92
Totals	315	260	83

Utah, Indiana, and Illinois, all sixteen states require various forms of local referenda.

The absence of authorizing legislation, however, does not preclude most legislatures from enacting specific city-county consolidations as legislative acts. Such, indeed, was the path followed successfully in consolidating Indianapolis-Marion County as well as, a century ago, in creating New York City.

Uniform state laws should be enacted to encourage city-county consolidation through local initiative. The desirable provisions of such laws would include

1. establishing a consolidation charter commission by action of city or county government or both;

TABLE 3.4
STATE LAWS REGARDING CITY-COUNTY CONSOLIDATION

State law	Number of states				
	South (16)	West (13)	Midwest (12)	Northeast (9)	Total USA (50)
Consolidation of cities and counties is authorized	5	7	4	0	16
Referendum and majority approval of each city affected is required	4	5	1	0	10
Referendum and majority approval of county is required	3	4	1	0	8
Referendum and majority approval of unincorporated area of county is required	2	1	0	0	3

2. authorizing the creation of urban and rural service districts (with different tax levels) within a consolidated government;
3. authorizing the inclusion of traditional county functions (assessor, clerk, and so on) in the consolidated government;
4. authorizing approval of the consolidated government by a single referendum of all affected voters (no single-jurisdiction veto).

Unifying local government in metro areas, however, is primarily a task for state government. There are too many obstacles at the local level, including entrenched officeholders, to rely on local initiative. For reforms to occur on a widespread scale, action must be taken by far-sighted and politically courageous governors and state legislators.

AUTHORIZE ANNEXATION

A second initiative needed by the states is to improve local annexation authority. For many small, relatively young metro areas, the central city's ability to annex urbanizing areas will be sufficient to maintain a basic unity of local government. Even in older, more built-up areas there are often opportunities for annexation that would benefit central cities. It is important to have good municipal annexation laws as tools to improve a city's elasticity.

Municipal annexation is authorized by general law in forty-one states (see Table 3.5). Once again, the Northeast lags: annexations are specifically authorized only in New Jersey and New York.

Many states, however, attach conditions that can severely inhibit a municipality's ability to annex. Thirty-three states allow the annexation process to be initiated by a petition of property owners in the area to be annexed. Usually the support of a majority or extraordinary majority of property owners is required. In half of these states, annexation can be initiated *only* by property owner petition—a very severe limitation placing a city's expansion at the mercy of suburban developers and residents. By contrast, twenty-four states allow annexation to be initiated by city ordinance or resolution.

In twenty-three states a referendum or majority approval of property owners in the area to be annexed is required—another tough hurdle except where large blocs of land are owned by a handful of pro-annexation developers. In ten states voters in the

TABLE 3.5
STATE LAWS REGARDING MUNICIPAL ANNEXATIONS

State law	Number of states				
	South (16)	West (13)	Midwest (12)	Northeast (9)	Total USA (50)
Municipal annexation is authorized by state law	15	12	12	2	41
Initiated by property owner petition	11	10	10	2	33
Initiated by city ordinance or resolution	12	5	7	0	24
Public hearing is required	7	7	5	1	20
Referendum and majority approval in city are required	5	1	3	1	10
Referendum or majority approval in area to be annexed is required	10	6	5	2	23
Approval of county governing authority is required	1	2	2	0	5

annexing city must approve the annexation—an invitation to opposition from no-growth advocates or minority political activists fearing dilution of minority voting power.

In Virginia, Nevada, Washington, Nebraska, and Ohio the affected county government must approve any municipal annexation. If the county fears loss of revenues, this could be a very significant obstacle to municipal expansion.

Faced with an expanding municipality, property owners should have rights. I believe, however, that state law should empower municipalities to initiate and carry out annexations while protecting property owners against any harm from such actions. State statutes should protect annexed property owners against increased taxes without commensurate increased services and unwarranted intrusion in rural lifestyles, absent significant urbanization. There should be a presumption, however, that annexation will serve the larger public interest.

In general terms, a model state annexation statute would

1. set forth the standards by which an annexation would be deemed to serve the general public interest;

2. authorize annexation to be initiated either by petition by landowners or resolution by city council;
3. require public hearings and due process;
4. authorize annexation to be consummated by council action alone; and
5. allow affected landowners the right of appeal to the state's District Court in the event landowners are aggrieved because annexation occurred despite their opposition or because their petition was rejected by the municipality.

LIMIT NEW MUNICIPALITIES

The ease or difficulty with which new municipalities are formed strongly affects the degree of fragmentation of urbanizing areas into multiple local governments. Virtually all states in the South, West, and Midwest set some limitations regarding minimum population, minimum area, or minimum ad valorem tax base (see Table 3.6). These limitations, however, tend to be modest. With the exception of New York, northeastern states are silent on the matter. In effect, the geopolitical map of New England, New York, and Pennsylvania is set in concrete.

Eighteen states require a minimum distance between the proposed and existing municipalities. (In New Mexico, for example,

TABLE 3.6
STATE LAWS REGARDING FORMING NEW MUNICIPALITIES

	Number of states				
State law	South (16)	West (13)	Midwest (12)	Northeast (9)	Total USA (50)
Limits are imposed on incorporation of new local government units	15	11	12	1	39
Minimum population is required	14	8	6	1	29
Minimum area is required	4	2	2	1	9
Minimum distance from existing units is required	9	5	4	0	18
Minimum ad valorem tax base is required	2	0	3	0	5

the distance is five miles.) In retrospect, perhaps this is the most useful requirement limiting the formation of new municipalities.

Requirements regarding minimum population, minimum area, and minimum ad valorem tax base should be considerably higher than prevailing standards. (In general, I believe in strengthening county government rather than proliferating the number of towns and small cities.) State law also ought to provide for a substantial zone around existing municipalities in which the existing government can veto the incorporation of new municipalities or other public bodies.

Finally, there ought to be different classes of municipalities based on size of population. Large cities ought to be given the presumptive authority over smaller cities to annex contested lands or even to absorb smaller cities in quasi-consolidation-type actions. Small municipalities, in turn, should be able to appeal such actions by large municipalities to the state's District Court.

PROMOTE PUBLIC PARTNERSHIPS

The fourth state-based initiative I want to discuss is promoting public partnerships. Short of reshaping the local political map, states can authorize or pursue functional policies to achieve some of the benefits of metro government. Thirty-nine states specifically authorize local governments to enter into joint powers or joint service agreements. These agreements allow local governments to band together to address problems that transcend local political boundaries. For the most part, joint powers or joint service agreements address infrastructure issues (for example, sewage treatment and air quality management) or "nonthreatening" service needs (for example, emergency medical services and services for senior citizens). They rarely touch the core of social and economic divisions within metro areas—housing, schools, and fiscal disparities.

There are creative exceptions, however. Minneapolis–St. Paul has a multicounty tax-sharing compact (see Box 3.3). In the Portland, Oregon, area, the state legislature and area voters have created a unique metro government (see Box 3.4). This multiprogram government, with its own elected officials and independent taxing powers, handles both a variety of infrastructure services and areawide land-use planning. The state legislature in Connecticut has recently enacted requirements for suburban

---

**Box 3.3 Tax-Base Sharing in the Twin Cities
Reduces Fiscal Disparities**

There has been only one significant experiment in the nation in metropolitan tax-base sharing. This is the fiscal disparities plan enacted by the Minnesota legislature in 1971.

The Twin Cities' Metropolitan Council thus describes the rationale for the Minneapolis-St. Paul plan:

> From a regional perspective the Twin Cities is one economy. Large commercial-industrial developments tend to concentrate in a few locations, drawing workers and clients from a market area that is larger than the city it is located in. Access to these concentrations, primarily highways, is a prime determinant of where these developments locate. Cities with such access are the ones most likely to get commercial-industrial development.
>
> Since the property tax is the primary source of local government revenues, certain types of development—office space, headquarters buildings, up-scale housing—are attractive because they typically generate more revenue than it costs to serve them. Not all cities can expect to attract such development, but most participate in financing the regional facilities serving these developments. The idea underlying tax-base sharing is to allow all cities to share in the commercial-industrial development that is, to a large extent, the result of the regional market and public investments made at the regional and state levels.[1]

Under the state law, the plan applies to 188 municipalities in the seven-county Twin Cities area. Since 1971, 40 percent of the

---

governments to participate in affordable housing programs (see Box 3.5).

Woodrow Wilson called the states "the laboratory of democracy." America's urban problem presents the states with their toughest challenge to live up to that honored billing.

Federal Government Initiatives

In any constitutional sense the federal government has no role in the way in which local governments are organized within the states. The Congress cannot, for example, just legislate the or-

increase in taxes from commercial-industrial property has been paid into a common pool. (A city's pre-1971 assessed valuation is exempted.) The pool is then redistributed among all 188 municipalities based on annual estimated population and how each city's per capita market value of property compares with the metrowide per capita value.

By 1991 the annual "fiscal disparities" fund amounted to $290.5 million, almost 31 percent of the region's $943 million in commercial-industrial assessed property valuation. Some 157 municipalities were net recipients; 31 were net contributors. The net contributors were primarily Twin Cities' major suburbs. Giant shopping malls, office towers, and garden-like industrial parks have sprouted along the interstate highways that cut through these suburbs or are adjacent to the suburban Minneapolis–St. Paul International Airport.

The largest net recipient in 1980, Minneapolis has become the largest net contributor. This transformation was fueled by the office boom downtown. Minneapolis's $19 million net contribution in 1991 represented 6.5 percent of its commercial-industrial tax capacity.

The tax-base sharing program is successfully reducing fiscal disparities between rich and poor communities. Among cities of 9,000 or more inhabitants, the ratio of richest community to poorest community would be 22 to 1, as measured by per capita commercial-industrial property value. The pioneering "fiscal disparities" program has reduced the ratio to 4 to 1.

1. This quotation and all data are from Metropolitan Council, Minneapolis, Minnesota, *Fiscal Disparities Discussion Paper* (April 16, 1991).

ganization of metropolitan governments. Federal policy, nevertheless, has had a decisive impact on the emergence of suburban America since World War II and on the corresponding decline of central cities.

- The Federal Housing Administration and the Veterans Administration have backed millions of low-interest mortgages for single-family homes in suburbia. Today the federal government's mortgage portfolio covers over 8 million homeowners—about 20 percent of all homes—with an outstanding principal of $400 billion.
- The U.S. Department of Transportation has made the auto-based suburbs possible. It has spent about $260 billion in fed-

Box 3.4 Portland's Unique Metro Government

We, the people of the Portland area metropolitan services district, in order to establish an elected, visible and accountable regional government that is responsive to the citizens of the region and works cooperatively with our local governments; that undertakes, as its most important services, planning and policy making to preserve and enhance the quality of life and the environment for ourselves and future generations; and that provides regional services needed and desired by the citizens in an efficient and effective manner, do ordain this charter for the Portland area metropolitan services district, to be known as Metro.

With that preamble, Portland area voters on November 3, 1992, adopted a "home rule" charter for the Portland Metropolitan Services District, established by the legislature in 1970. This vote in 1992 was the most recent step in the evolution of a unique approach to metro government in the Portland area—now three counties and twenty-four municipalities.

Metrowide special units of government are common. Portland's Metro is uncommon in the wide scope of its functions: solid waste collection, recycling, and disposal; transportation planning and allocation of federal highway and road funds; regional air and water quality programs; operation of the regional zoo; and construction and operation of the new $85 million Oregon Convention Center. Metro also is unique because it is the only directly elected regional government in the United States. Under the guidance of its elected, seven-member, nonpartisan commission and elected executive officer, it has a $225 million annual budget and 1,200 employees.

In the new charter the area's citizenry affirmed that regional planning is Metro's "primary function." The charter charges Metro with developing a fifty-year "Future Vision" and a "Regional Framework Plan." The charter then empowers the Metro Council to adopt ordinances to require local comprehensive plans and zoning regulations to comply with the Regional Framework Plan, to adjudicate inconsistencies between regional and local plans, and to change inconsistent local land use standards and procedures. Metro also is empowered to carry out any other functions or services assigned to it by the state legislature or approved by the voters of the Metro district.

After decades of patient development, Portland's Metro is a model structure for multicounty regional governance.

eral aid for roads and highways (about half in urban areas). This has been about five times the amount of city-oriented federal aid for mass transit.

- The federal treasury forgoes $37 billion a year in tax revenues because mortgage interest (on homes largely in the suburbs) is deductible. By comparison, federal tax law provides $1 billion a year in tax credits to encourage city-oriented, moderate-income apartment construction. Thus, even in an era of ever shrinking federal aid, the government sustains the suburban impetus.

If, as I believe, the "action" is really with state and local governments—and with citizens as state and local voters—what can the federal government do to stimulate movement toward metropolitan government? Possible actions fall into two categories: incentives for metropolitan reorganization and new requirements on the use of federal grants-in-aid.

INCENTIVES FOR METROPOLITAN REORGANIZATION

"Incentives" is a euphemism for federal money—either dollars spent or taxes not paid. Re-energizing the American economy, controlling health-care costs, and systematically reducing the federal deficit must be the paramount federal goals. Proposing incentives to promote metropolitan government is politically hazardous and intellectually troubling. I am certainly prepared to see metropolitan government advocated at state and local levels without federal incentives as long as the federal government stops doing active harm to the cause.

Nevertheless, I believe that the urban problem is central to our declining economic competitiveness. For America to revive its economic and social health, solving the urban problem is an essential component. Placing local governments on a sound financial basis, reducing racial and economic segregation, invigorating areawide economic growth—these are outcomes for which it is worth considering federal incentives.

The size of the problem is huge. Over 190 million people live in metro areas—almost 80 percent of the country's population. Only three percent live in areas served now by metro governments (see Table 3.1). To be effective, any incentives would have to be significant, and, when successful, would have a major impact on the federal budget. I have no desire to have my pro-

Box. 3.5 Connecticut Legislature
Champions Affordable Housing

In per capita income Connecticut is the country's wealthiest state. Its metro areas, however, rank ninth in racial segregation and first in economic segregation. Connecticut's housing patterns are partly to blame. Its central cities have been dominated by rental properties. (Hartford's residents, for example, are 80 percent renters.) Suburban towns have been oriented toward owner-occupied homes at towering prices.

High housing costs have had undeniable negative consequences. Many public employees (police officers, firefighters, teachers) cannot afford to live in the communities they serve. And many children cannot afford to live in the communities where they were raised.

As a result, the Connecticut General Assembly has passed a package of initiatives to stimulate more affordable housing.

To counter exclusionary zoning, the legislature explicitly authorized towns to adopt "inclusionary zoning" practices. For example, "density bonuses" allow developers to build more housing units per acre than local zoning would normally allow if they also build some affordable units.

To put enforcement teeth behind this policy, the General Assembly enacted in 1989 the Affordable Housing Land-Use Appeals Procedure. Under the new procedure, if a town council rejects a developer's affordable housing proposal, the developer can challenge the local ruling in state court. The burden of proof would be on the town council to prove that its reasons for rejecting the project "clearly outweigh the need for affordable housing." In effect, the legislature established the area's need for affordable housing as the primary public interest to be served and shifted the burden of proof from developer to town council.

Although suits can originate from communities throughout the

posals generate headlines such as "Multibillion-Dollar Federal Program Advocated to Promote Metropolitan Government" (*New York Times*) or "$$Big Bucks for Big Brother!!" (*New York Post*). But that phrase—"when successful"—is the key. The incentives I am suggesting cost nothing unless and until they are successful. Dollars are paid out or taxes forgone only when the desired goal—a metro government—is achieved. In other words, the "incentive" would actually be a "reward" for actual accomplishment.

state, appeals can be heard only by the state superior court in Hartford-New Britain. The legislation urged that cases be assigned to a "small number of judges so that a consistent body of expertise can be developed." The first half dozen appeals have all been heard by the same judge—with findings in each case supporting the affordable housing proposal.

Connecticut's law is not going to produce affordable housing on every village lane. First, the income ceiling for buying or renting affordable housing is set at 80 percent of an area's median income (about $29,000 for a four-person family statewide in 1990). Mortgage payments or monthly rentals cannot exceed 30 percent of family income. Second, a developer's project proposal can qualify if as little as 20 percent of the units are priced as affordable housing. Finally, communities where "assisted housing" already exceeds 10 percent of the housing supply are exempted. (Only about 25 of Connecticut's 169 towns meet or exceed this standard.) Also exempted are communities actively participating in Connecticut's Housing Partnership Program or Regional Fair Housing Compact Pilot Program.

Despite these qualifications, the Affordable Housing Land-Use Appeals Procedure should encourage racial integration in Connecticut. As a Connecticut attorney notes, "The unequal distribution of wealth and resources caused in part by towns' exclusionary land use decisions . . . created an imbalance between the housing needs of low-income, urban minorities and the housing opportunities of their more affluent, white, suburban neighbors. Opening up the suburbs to the full range of economic classes will . . . promote racial dispersal."[1]

1. Quoted in Melinda Westbrook, "Connecticut's New Affordable Housing Appeals Procedure Assaulting the Presumptive Validity of Land Use Decisions," *Connecticut Bar Journal* (June 1992). Other information cited in this box has been drawn from this source.

Because federal tax dollars would be on the line, I would add three requirements to help ensure that metro government achieves the desired social impact. First, to qualify for federal incentives, a metro government should adopt a jurisdiction-wide plan to stimulate affordable housing. Second, it should reorganize the local public housing authority on a jurisdiction-wide basis. Rent-subsidy programs should immediately be implemented in all areas, and plans to build future public housing projects should be adopted on a small-unit, scattered-site basis.

Third, a metro government should implement an aggressive fair housing and fair employment practices compliance program either through a metro government agency or state human rights agency (if the state agency has a record of effectiveness).

Now, having set the guidelines, what specific incentives would make sense? I would suggest three different kinds: personal-income tax incentives, tax-exempt bond incentives, and federal grant-in-aid bonuses.

— *Personal-income tax incentives.*   Taxpayers now can deduct state and local income taxes and property taxes from federal taxable income. To encourage local voter support of metro government, the Congress could amend the federal income tax code to provide a "bonus" deduction for taxes paid to support metro governments.

For example, for taxes paid to a Class III metropolitan government, taxpayers might receive a 60-percent additional deduction; to Class II, an 80-percent additional deduction; and to Class I, a 100-percent additional deduction. Thus, if a taxpayer currently pays $1,000 in taxes to a suburban county, if that county consolidated with its central city (achieving, say, Class I metro government status), the taxpayer could deduct not $1,000 (as in the past), but $2,000 against federal tax liability. This would result in a real savings to the federal taxpayer of $280 from his or her current tax bill (an additional $1,000 deduction multiplied by a 28-percent marginal tax rate).

If, furthermore, the new consolidated government were to seek the taxpayer's support for a $200 tax increase, the real cost to that taxpayer would be only $88. The other $112 would be recaptured by the taxpayer in federal taxes not paid ($200 x 200 percent x 28 percent = $112).

Two economic objections to this proposal are also its political strengths. First, deducting state and local taxes is highly regressive since only about 20 percent of all federal taxpayers (generally from higher-income groups) itemize their deductions. These are precisely the taxpayers—often upper-income suburbanites—whose support for metro government must be encouraged.

Second, levels of state and local taxation among the states differ. New York, for example, is a high-tax state; Texas is a low-tax state. Thus, federal rewards for metropolitanization might flow proportionally more to New Yorkers than to Texans. However, city-county consolidation is more easily achieved in Texas than New York because of Texas's larger-sized counties, more limited number of municipalities, and lower city-suburb racial "gradients." In effect, on achieving a metro government, residents of the Syracuse, Rochester, or Buffalo areas would be rewarded more because metropolitanization would have been harder to achieve than in Houston or Dallas or Fort Worth.

Tax-exempt bond incentives.   The federal treasury already subsidizes local governments by allowing the interest earned from local government bonds to be tax free. To promote metropolitanization, the Congress could add an incentive in the form of an actual federal tax credit for metro government bonds. For example, the credit could be equal to 15 percent of interest earnings for bonds from Class III metro governments; 20 percent for Class II; and 25 percent for Class I.

This proposal also can be criticized for its regressive impact on the tax system. Tax exempt bonds are purchased by those who have large amounts of capital to invest, who have substantial federal tax liability, and who are looking for low-risk, long-term investments. Yet again, in political terms, these are exactly the individual and institutional investors whom we want to ally with metropolitanization.

Federal grants-in-aid bonuses.   Although much atrophied from past levels, federal funds distributed to state and local governments by formula allocation now total $60 billion (excluding $60 billion in medicaid assistance). Another incentive for metropolitanization would be to add an overriding bonus to grants-in-aid formulas for metro governments. Formula grants to metro governments (and to state governments for pass-through grants) might be increased by 15 percent for Class III governments; 20 percent for Class II governments; and 25 percent for Class I governments.

FISCAL IMPACT OF INCENTIVES

Purely on the basis of population coverage, only forty-eight governments representing 3.3 percent of the nation's population already fulfill my definitions as metro governments. For even these to qualify for federal incentives, they would have to meet the additional qualifications proposed: a jurisdiction-wide, affordable housing plan, a jurisdiction-wide housing assistance program, and a jurisdiction-wide fair housing/fair employment program.

Assuming these additional standards are met, it would be tempting to reward these communities (and their taxpayers) for good works already achieved. Incentives, however, should promote future action. Therefore, the incentives I have described should reward only future actions taken to further metro government. Already qualified metro governments ought not to be rewarded unless they undertake additional actions to extend their jurisdictional coverage (over, for example, an additional 5 percent of their metro area population above 1990 levels). By this standard, the only metro government that should be allowed to qualify immediately would be Anchorage, Alaska—the nation's only Class I, or 100-percent coverage, metropolitan government. (Anchorage accounts for approximately 0.1 percent of the nation's population.)

Table 3.7, which is based on Table 3.2, provides a rough estimate of the fiscal impact of federal incentives. It assumes that every central city is successfully consolidated with its host urban county or, conversely, that the host county becomes the single, all-purpose unit of government.

Many such areas may not be seen as in trouble. Should they be rewarded for fixing something that "ain't broke"? The answer is yes. Preventive medicine is the cheapest policy in the

TABLE 3.7
POTENTIAL FISCAL IMPACT OF FEDERAL INCENTIVES
IF ALL CITY–SINGLE COUNTY UNIFICATIONS OCCUR
(BILLIONS OF DOLLARS)

Incentive Program	Current cost	Incentive factor	Fiscal impact
Local income tax deduction bonus	$27.50	0.3636	$10.00
Property tax deduction bonus	13.30	0.3636	4.84
Tax-exempt bond credit	35.40*	0.0909	3.22
Federal grants-in-aid bonus	60.00	0.0909	5.45
Total fiscal impact			$23.51

*Estimated bond interest earned.

long run. All areas, including nonproblem communities, should be encouraged to put their governmental houses in order.

What would happen if all cities successfully consolidated with their urban counties? Metropolitan governments would be created in 83 percent of America's urban areas, covering 55 percent of the nation's urban population. The fiscal impact of these incentives on the federal budget—$18 billion a year in tax relief to individual taxpayers and bond holders and $5 billion in additional grants-in-aid to metro government—would be over $23 billion a year. That is an enormous amount: it would equal the cost of another half dozen B-2 bombers, another half dozen Trident submarines, and equipping and maintaining two armored divisions for a year!

NEW REQUIREMENTS ON FEDERAL GRANTS-IN-AID

Congress recently has created new metropolitan planning requirements for the Clean Air Act and the Intermodal Surface Transportation Efficiency Act (see Box 3.6). The impact of the Clean Air Act amendments is primarily regulatory; only $163 million in Federal Air Pollution Control Assistance grants nationwide is conditioned upon meeting the metropolitan planning requirements.

Transportation planning, however, is another matter. Federally designated "metropolitan planning organizations" (typically, voluntary Councils of Government) must plan and allocate federal transportation funds in an integrated fashion areawide. Between highway and transit aid, the amount of money at issue is about $10 billion a year.

An examination of federal grants-in-aid allocated by formula reveals relatively few targets of opportunity for metropolitan planning requirements. The Department of Housing and Urban Development's (HUD) Community Development Block Grants ($2.086 billion) and the Department of Labor's Job Training Partnership Act ($1.461 billion) are possibilities. Most federal assistance, however, is channeled through state health and welfare agencies that function apart from local government.

The federal government, nevertheless, could try three new initiatives. First, it could give planning and technical assistance to state and local governments to develop metro government proposals. Frankly, I am unenthusiastic about this approach.

Box 3.6 Ice Tea: The Fed's New Regional Brew

After languishing at the federal level throughout the 1980s, regionalism was revived in 1991 when Congress passed the Intermodal Surface Transportation Efficiency Act (ISTEA).

Since 1973 local governments have been involved in planning the use of certain federal funds for transportation. In the judgment of the National Association of Regional Councils, ISTEA "marks a radical and visionary transformation in the nation's transportation policy."[1]

ISTEA authorizes $151 billion over six years (fiscal years 1992-97) for highway and transit assistance. The key change is the greater discretion afforded local officials in the use of federal funds.

In the past local planning was largely limited to prioritizing laundry lists of projects within narrow, federally prescribed program allocations. Under ISTEA, "Metropolitan Planning Organizations" (MPOs) for all urbanized areas with 200,000 or more residents will have broad discretion to allocate lump-sum federal funds among road, bridge, and transit projects.

About half of all MPOs are "regional councils," voluntary consortia of local governments with a variety of program interests beyond transportation planning. Other MPOs are regional economic development organizations, transportation planning agencies, or arms of state highway departments.

"ISTEA's implementation must not degenerate into a turf war—states, MPOs, and local governments all seeking primacy," warns the National Association of Regional Councils. "We must develop true collaborative approaches to planning and programming these funds."[2]

Transportation networks help determine how and where people live, work, and play. Yet transportation planning rarely excites passions (except, of course, when a new highway is planned through existing neighborhoods). ISTEA can be an important building block toward greater regional integration.

1. National Association of Regional Councils, *Regional Reporter* 3 (January 1992):1
2. National Association of Regional Councils, "ISTEA of 1991: A Strategic Overview." Memorandum [1992]:1-2.

The federal government is broke. State government ought to shoulder the up-front costs of addressing what is primarily its responsibility. Where you stand, however, depends on where you sit. A federal spoonful of sugar may be necessary to start the medicine going down.

Second, the federal government could rethink the whole administration of the nationwide public housing program. Federal assistance flows to local public housing authorities in the form of construction grants, operating subsidies, and rent supplement subsidies. Local public housing authorities, however, are usually agencies of specific city governments. They have little authority or incentive to operate across jurisdictional lines—either to construct or operate public housing projects or, despite recent "portability" provisions, to provide rent subsidies to city residents who may opt for housing elsewhere in the area.

The federal court-ordered Gautreaux Project in the Chicago area has demonstrated the striking effectiveness of metrowide jurisdiction (see Box 3.7). Albuquerque's almost metrowide housing authority is another example (see Box 3.8).

The federal government should adopt a Gautreaux-type strategy for public housing on a nationwide scale. A key would be to break out of the single-jurisdiction straitjacket of existing public housing authorities. Congress should legislate new requirements immediately to put public housing authorities on a metrowide basis. Agreements could be reached either with consortia of local governments (politically difficult to achieve) or with state governments as a new federal-state system. In the event of unbending political resistance at state and local levels, the federal government should enter into direct arrangements with areawide nonprofit agencies to operate the federal public housing program directly.

Finally, the federal government can provide intellectual leadership, spurring growing national recognition of the need to reorganize local government. HUD could turn its research agenda toward city-suburb relations and the other issues raised by my analysis. HUD, like social workers toward their welfare clients, is long on sympathy and red tape and short on money. Often the captive of its constituents, HUD's traditional types of intervention in the lives of cities will not make much difference.

A more creative and intellectual approach is needed. During the 1970s the U.S. Advisory Commission on Intergovernmental

---

Box 3.7 From Failure in the Ghetto to Success in the Suburbs

The Gautreaux Project has drawn national attention by demonstrating that public housing tenants in inner cities can succeed simply by getting out of bad neighborhoods into better neighborhoods. Named for public-housing tenant activist Dorothy Gautreaux, the program began in 1976 when the federal courts found the Chicago Housing Authority (CHA) guilty of racial discrimination. One remedy the courts ordered was to subsidize moving public housing families out of CHA projects and into private rental housing elsewhere in Chicago or anywhere in Chicago's six-county suburban area.

Since 1976 over 4,700 families have participated in the program, administered by the Leadership Council for Metropolitan Open Communities, a court-appointed nonprofit organization. One-third of the families remained in Chicago; two-thirds moved to Chicago's suburbs.

James E. Rosenbaum, professor of sociology at Northwestern University, did a follow-up study of the "city movers" and "suburban movers."[1] Both showed the same socioeconomic profile entering the program: typically a Black, female head of household, receiving welfare assistance, with two or three children. Of the suburban-mover mothers, 64 percent were working compared with 51 percent for city-mover mothers. Of the suburban-mover children, 95 percent graduated from their suburban sys-

---

Relations (ACIR) was a constant source of provocative recommendations affecting the federal-state-local system. During the conservative decade of the 1980s, however, the ACIR eschewed practically any involvement in the complex cauldron of racial and class issues shaping urban America. A revitalized ACIR could play a key role in focusing renewed attention on metropolitan disparities and intergovernmental reform.

The best public policy "bully pulpit" is the White House. President Bill Clinton will have numerous meetings with delegations of mayors petitioning Uncle Sam for help. And he will respond as much as the head of a debt-ridden government can respond. But he needs to promote new ways of thinking about old problems. What would be the effect of the president responding to the mayors something like this:

tems compared with a graduation rate of 80 percent of city movers from Chicago schools. Fifty-four percent of suburban movers had continued their education (27 percent in four-year colleges) compared with 21 percent of city movers (4 percent in four-year colleges). Seventy-five percent of suburban-mover youth were working (21 percent for hourly wages of $6.50 or better); by contrast, 41 percent of city-mover youth had a job (5 percent at $6.50 or better per hour).

"Pessimistic predictions of 'culture of poverty' models are not supported," Rosenbaum concluded after completing his study. "The early experiences of low-income blacks do not prevent them from benefitting from suburban moves."

One participant in the Gautreaux Project summed up her experience in this way: "A housing project deteriorates you. You don't want to do anything. Living in the suburbs made me feel that I'm worth something. I can do anything I want to do if I get up and try it."

1. James E. Rosenbaum, "Black Pioneers—Do Their Moves to the Suburbs Increase Economic Opportunity for Mothers and Children?" in Federal National Mortgage Association (Fannie Mae), *Housing Policy Debate*, 2: 1213.

Outcomes for both suburban movers and city stayers were presumably superior to those for households remaining in many of Chicago's high-rise public housing projects.

Well, mayors, I want to assure you that my administration will do all we can to help. But let me ask you a question. Now your cities sit in the middle of some of the wealthiest urban areas in the country. What can *you* do to get more help from your neighbors and start solving some of these problems without relying so much on Washington? Why don't you think about that some and come back to me with a plan.

Of course, most big city mayors do not have the power to achieve such solutions on their own. But they are not even *thinking* along these lines.

Prodding such thinking is cheap for a president. It costs the federal treasury nothing. It may cost the president some initial political capital. But capital hoarded is valueless. It must be invested to be productive. No American president since Lyndon

---

**Box 3.8 Public Housing Promotes
Economic Integration in Albuquerque**

In sharp contrast with many communities, in Albuquerque, public housing helps promote economic integration. The reason is three city policies that have shaped the public housing program from its inception.

First, build only small projects. No housing project exceeds sixty family units.

Second, consciously scatter the projects in all areas of the city. There are small projects located in eight of the city's ten high school attendance zones.

Third, promote economically mixed rental housing in all areas of the city. This allows a geographically diversified rent subsidy program. Rent subsidy families are scattered among all the residential zip code areas within the city limits. The most affected zip code has only 20 percent of all subsidized households; the least affected still is home to 3 percent of the assisted families.

The city of Albuquerque has 80 percent of the metro population within its city limits. Thus, the Albuquerque Housing Authority operates a nearly metrowide program.

Johnson has seriously invested presidential capital in pushing this nation to deal with the roots of inequality.

Citizen Initiatives

Brainstorming about federal initiatives is very seductive. It can lead readers (and authors) astray. Reorganizing local government is primarily a task for initiative and hard work at state and local levels.

Wherever major structural reforms have been accomplished, there has been a civic movement at the core of the effort. Typically such movements have been broad-based coalitions of citizens concerned about improving government from across the metro area, leading business and labor interests, civic organizations, and (less frequently) key local political leaders. In each of my case studies of city-county consolidation, such a metrowide coalition has been the engine of reform, whether the arena for change has been the state legislature or the ballot box.

A national leader in promoting voluntary civic action has been the National Civic League. Founded in 1894, the National Civic League helped nurture the so-called "good government" movement in the early decades of this century. Out of citizen reform coalitions in many communities arose sweeping changes in local government in many states, including adoption of the commission-manager system by many local governments and the evolution of career civil service systems.

For more than sixty years regional governance has been a focus of the National Civic League. In recent years the National Civic League has supported the emergence of what have been called "regional civic organizations." Their advantages are many, a National Civic League memo has noted.

> . . . [W]hereas various attempts to expand regional government—for example, through city-county consolidations, annexations, and federations—have succeeded with declining frequency over the past twenty years, informal regional governance—in the form of voluntary cooperative arrangements between local governments, and in regional agenda setting efforts sponsored by civic organizations and non-profit planning organizations—has flourished.
>
> Informal governance often works where government fails because its structure is typically loose, its membership inclusive, and its strategies dependent on building cooperative coalitions. Whereas government is perceived as operating through a top-down approach to problems and imposing requirements on people, informal governance operates bottom-up by gathering authority from the people it can convince of its cause.
>
> What is most impressive is that informal governance approaches to regionalism appear to be better able to address the difficult problems that elected officials either lack the courage or the will to address, for example, fair share housing, comprehensive regional land use and transportation planning, revenue base sharing, and tax increases."[2]

Among the most active regional civic organizations in the nation are the San Francisco Bay area's Bay Vision 2020 (see Box 3.9); the Community Cooperation Task Force of Metropolitan Dayton; and Confluence St. Louis. The Community Cooperation Task Force, an initiative of the Dayton area's Chamber of Commerce, has established a countywide economic development fund, shared by all municipalities and replenished by a tax-sharing fund financed by the incremental taxes generated by countywide development. Confluence St. Louis is a 1,100-mem-

Box 3.9 Bay Vision 2020 Promotes Regional Reform

In the San Francisco Bay region, uncoordinated actions of local governments made comprehensive transportation and land-use planning virtually impossible. Large corporations needed a predictable framework for investment and improved competitiveness. Environmentalists needed compact, orderly development that would preserve open space and reduce dependence on automobiles. Often at each other's throats, large corporations and environmentalists finally got together in late 1989. With the endorsement of local elected officials, they joined forces to initiate a year-long "visioning" process: Bay Vision 2020.

Convened by an industrial group (the Bay Area Council) and an environmental group (the Greenbelt Alliance), thirty-one commissioners from industry, government, universities, and nonprofit interest groups met to discuss regional reform. They proposed a new Regional Commission that would prepare a regional plan and administer the air quality district, the transportation district, and a fair-share housing program.

Bay Vision 2020 drafted state legislation that would establish the proposed Regional Commission on a trial, three-year basis. Within that period the Regional Commission would have to develop and achieve local government consensus on a regional plan. If successful, the Regional Commission would be reauthorized at the end of the three years.

The objective of Bay Vision 2020 "was not to become a regional planning authority but to put in place a public authority that local governments on their own lacked the will (and possibly the capacity) to conceive."[1]

1. National Civic League, "Regional Civic Governance: Emerging Organizational Structure and Strategies: A Proposal by the National Civic League," *National Civic Review*, August 1991, p. 3.

ber regional civic organization that works across municipal, county, and state boundaries to improve the quality of life in the St. Louis metro area. To date, Confluence St. Louis has issued nine reports addressing issues ranging from solid waste management to race relations. These reports have spurred new legislation as well as private sector efforts.

As vehicles for sustained reform, voluntary citizen organizations probably do not have the multidecade staying power of formal structural reforms. Nevertheless, they are precisely what is needed to build political support for metro government. The new administration in Washington will not be bankrupt intellectually, but it will be bankrupt fiscally. It will not have the luxury of federal dollars as leverage to encourage local reform.

Unprodded by citizen pressure, few state houses show any willingness to shoulder the tough political task of metropolitan reorganization. Mayors, city councillors, and county commissioners are too caught up in short-term pressures for survival and too politically comfortable with existing divisions. The National Civic League has correctly noted that local governments "have assiduously avoided policies and arrangements which would result in sharing the social burdens of inner city populations or otherwise breaching the social insulation of the suburbs from their central city problems."[3]

Such avoidance must stop. Regional civic organizations must become the engines of change.

Notes

1. A special definition must be created for the gigantic, multistate New York–northwestern New Jersey–Long Island CMSA. Within the New York portion, the New York PMSA, Nassau–Suffolk PMSA, and Orange County PMSA should be considered as one combined area. Within this area a Class III metropolitan government should serve 75 percent or more; and a Class II, 90 percent or more. The New Jersey and Connecticut components can be treated under the regular definitions.

2. National Civic League, "Regional Civic Goverance: Emerging Organizational Structure and Strategies: A Proposal by the National Civic League," *National Civic Review* (August 1991): 3.

3. Ibid.

Chapter IV

Conclusions and Recommendations

What is missing from current debate over urban policy is any willingness to attack the urban problem as a matter of racial and economic segregation. Liberals appeal for large-scale federal aid for social welfare and economic development programs in the inner cities. This is the Big Buck Strategy. Conservatives talk about inner city enterprise zones, public housing "perestroika," and "empowerment." This is the Big Bootstrap Strategy.

At heart, Big Buckers and Big Bootstrappers are selling the same idea: quarantine "them" in inner city ghettos and barrios away from "us" and help "them" build from within—with money or moral incentives. Both ideological camps believe that separate can be made equal, or at least equal enough to be tolerable.

"Separate but equal" cannot work. It has never worked. Ghettos and barrios create and perpetuate an urban underclass. *Bad communities defeat good programs.* Successful clients of social programs typically move away. As a result, in inner cities, individual success does not translate into community success. Life in ghettos and barrios gets worse. Even with flourishing downtowns, inner cities decline. Inner-city neighborhoods deteriorate as places to raise families. With shrinking tax bases, city budgets are unable to meet rising social needs.

Enterprise zones, community development banks, nonprofit inner-city housing developments—all the tools of "empowerment"—are not futile efforts. They will produce some new businesses, some new jobs, some new homes, and some revitalized neighborhoods. They will be more effective, however, if carried out within a framework of actions to bring down the walls between city and suburb. Absent efforts at reunification, such programs will be unable to reverse the downward slide of the inner cities.

121

National urban policy, state-by-state urban policy, and area-by-area urban policy must focus on breaking up ghettos and barrios. Urban policy must systematically help ghetto and barrio residents become integrated into the entire metropolitan area. A revived middle class in the cities—not a "bucked-up" or "boot-strapped-up" urban poor—must be the leavening yeast of inner city revival.

Urban underclass behavior substantially dissolves with integration into the larger community. Individual poverty and dependency or individual acts of crime certainly do not disappear, but they lack critical mass to blight whole communities. Within all metro areas the proportion of poor minorities, if dispersed, is not so large as to overwhelm middle-class culture. It is the very isolation and hyperconcentration of poor minorities that overwhelms *them* individually. Neither poor people nor inner cities can succeed if they are cast into the sociological equivalents of giant public housing projects.

Throughout history cities have been the arena of opportunity and upward mobility. In America the "city" has been redefined since World War II. The real city is now the whole urban area—city and suburb—the metropolitan area. Redeeming inner cities and the urban underclass requires reintegration of city and suburb.

This is the toughest political issue in American society. It goes right to the heart of Americans' fears about race and class. There will be no short-term, politically comfortable solutions.

The organization of metro areas into local governments has greatly affected the degree of racial and economic segregation. Within their expanding municipal boundaries, elastic cities have captured much of the growth of the suburbs. Elastic cities minimize city-suburb disparities, thereby lessening the separations between racial and economic groups.

Inelastic cities, in the battle over middle-class America, have lost to their suburbs. Some never even fought the good fight. Whatever the success of their downtowns as regional employment centers, inelastic city neighborhoods have increasingly housed most of the metro area's poor Blacks and Hispanics.

How can responsibility for poor minorities be made a metropolitan-wide responsibility? How can all jurisdictions—city and suburb—assume a "fair share"?

Traditionally, the primary purpose of regional cooperation among local governments has been the delivery of public services. Regional arrangements usually avoid policies and programs that share the social burdens of inner-city residents. Yet this is the heart of the challenge. Areawide compacts on transportation planning, solid waste management, sewage treatment, and air quality management may be "good government," but they address the urban problem only if they attack racial and economic segregation.

For many small and medium-sized metro areas, the surest way to avoid or reverse patterns of racial and economic segregation is to create metro governments. This can be achieved by expanding the central city through aggressive annexation policies, by consolidating the city and county, or by fully empowering county government and abolishing or reducing the role of municipalities.

For larger, more complex metro areas, metro government may be neither politically feasible nor administratively desirable. Larger government is not necessarily more efficient government. At any scale, efficiency is largely a function of good management. Given the bureaucratic impulse of many large systems, metro government may be less efficient and less responsive as a deliverer of services than smaller governments.

It is not important that local residents have their garbage picked up by a metrowide garbage service or their parks managed by a metrowide parks and recreation department. It is important that all local governments pursue common policies that will diminish racial and economic segregation. The following four policies are essential:

1. "fair share" housing policies (supported by planning and zoning policies) that will encourage low- and moderate-income housing in all jurisdictions;
2. fair employment and fair housing policies to ensure full access by minorities to the job and housing markets;
3. housing assistance policies to disperse low-income families to small-unit, scattered-site housing projects and to rent-subsidized private rental housing throughout a diversified metro housing market; and
4. tax-sharing arrangements that will offset tax-base disparities between the central city and its suburbs.

In baldest terms, sustained success requires moving poor people from bad city neighborhoods to good suburban neighborhoods and moving dollars from relatively wealthy suburban governments to poorer city governments. The long-term payoff will be an overall reduction in poverty, dependency, and crime areawide, and "prosperous cities [which] are the key to vital regional economies and to safe and healthy suburbs."[1]

State government must play the leading role. Local government is the creature of state government, which sets the ground rules for local initiative and can create new local governments and merge old ones. Furthermore, governors and state legislators can and do act as metrowide policymakers. State government also plays an increasingly important role in revenue sharing for local government. With the purse comes additional power (and responsibility) to make the organization of metro areas more rational and equitable.

State government must act. It must

1. improve annexation laws to facilitate continuous central city expansion into urbanizing areas;
2. enact laws to encourage city-county consolidation through local initiative or to reorganize local government by direct state statute;
3. empower county governments with all municipal powers so that they can act as de facto metro governments, where appropriate;
4. require all local governments in metro areas to have "fair share" affordable housing laws; and
5. establish metrowide tax-sharing arrangements for local governments or utilize state aid as a revenue-equalizing mechanism.

As I stated earlier, reorganizing local government is primarily a task for initiative and hard work at the state and local levels. There are key roles, however, for the federal government. Since World War II the federal government's "urban policy" has been "suburban policy." It is past time for the federal government to deal with the consequences of its handiwork in terms of helping bridge the city-suburb gap.

First, the federal government should focus federal research and evaluation on integrating poor minorities into social mainstream communities. This is preferable to aiding them through social programs for socially isolated inner city areas.

Second, the federal government should utilize the U.S. Advisory Commission on Intergovernmental Relations more actively.

The commission could help the National Governors Association, National Conference of State Legislators, National Association of Counties, National League of Cities, and other organizations promote metropolitan reorganization and develop model state laws.

Third, each federal program should be reviewed to see whether it increases or diminishes racial and economic segregation. This could be done by the Domestic Council or similar White–House–led body. Executive regulations or congressional amendments should then modify federal programs to diminish segregating effects and increase integrating effects.

Fourth, the federal government should initiate a major reform of the federal public housing program. Local public housing authorities should be made metrowide and should emphasize the use of rent-subsidy vouchers to provide access for the city poor to rental housing throughout metro areas. Housing the urban poor in high-density, inner-city public housing projects is patently destructive and should be ended as soon as possible.

Fifth, enforcement of federal laws on fair employment and fair housing should be made more vigorous.

Finally, the federal government should determine whether public and private policies that result in economic segregation, because of their high correlation with racial segregation, are *de facto* violations of federal civil rights laws.

President Clinton has set as his priorities revitalizing the economy, controlling health care costs, and reducing the federal budget deficit. Although these are daunting tasks, there are still a greater national consensus and more policy tools at hand to address these priorities than there are consensus and tools to attack the schisms between city and suburb that lie at the core of America's urban problem.

Sustained change will require a grassroots movement like the civil rights movement or the environmental movement. This new movement will be tougher to begin. The civil rights movement in the 1960s mobilized moral outrage against Jim Crow laws. The environmental movement in the 1970s reflected compelling concern with human survival on a despoiled planet. But for the movement against urban segregation to get off the ground in the 1990s, a climate of perception, a climate of support, and a climate of change must be created.

Over 80 percent of all minorities now live in America's metropolitan areas. A racially equitable society can be achieved only if urban America is changed. Conversely, solving the problems of cities requires addressing the city-suburb schisms that have developed since World War II.

This is a journey on which few may initially choose to embark. But consider some of the alternative choices.

In an increasingly global economy would we choose to sacrifice the talent and productivity of inner city residents and burden society with growing costs of dependency and social disruption?

In a capital-scarce society would we choose to discard the tremendous investment in the inner cities?

In a world of fragile interdependence would we choose to have the suburbs survive as independent and prosperous communities while the inner cities collapse at the metropolitan core?

In a world in which the technology of violence can touch anyone, would we choose to live in a garrison state where police power tries to seal off the have-nots from the haves?

These "choices" suggest where the racial and economic segregation of urban America is leading. The crisis requires not just urban aid or even a true "urban policy" but a commitment to a spirit of shared sacrifice and renewal. The crisis requires exchanging the old politics of exclusion for a new politics of inclusion. It will test whether or not the American people can develop a new spirit of community.

Afterword

"You may have shifted from a theme of cities without suburbs to suburbs with incidental cities," commented my colleague Hank Savitch after reviewing an earlier draft of this book.

> Your central argument is that cities 'succeed' only if they continue to absorb suburbs, which you see as America's preferred lifestyle. City survival ought not be so dependent upon imitating suburban patterns. How can cities become viable again within a metropolitan environment? Frankly, I believe that cities do have different roles to play.

His comments brought me up short. I love old-fashioned, bustling downtowns, and I love the old apartment buildings and town houses, nearby shops, tree-lined streets, mini-parks, buses, and subways of good urban neighborhoods. There is nothing sadder than a city that undertakes a redevelopment project that looks and functions like a suburban office park and shopping mall.

As mayor I often spoke of Albuquerque as "a giant suburb in search of a city." Albuquerque had all the suburban lifestyle its advocates could possibly want, I suggested. Albuquerque needed to strengthen its urban character. With modest success and much controversy, I promoted downtown Albuquerque as a center of business, government, entertainment, and the arts.

Having returned to Washington, D.C., we live again within the District of Columbia in a condominium twelve minutes from the White House. A Metro bus stop is at the front door and a city park at the back door. Yet the District of Columbia is today only 15 percent of the population of the 4-million-person Washington Metropolitan Area, even before the census experts merged it with the 2.5-million-person Baltimore Metropolitan Area in 1992 to create the nation's fourth largest urban region.

Twenty years ago Washingtonians never went to Baltimore.

127

There was nothing there. Today Baltimore's spectacular Inner Harbor is a standard weekend attraction. In the inaugural season for the wonderful Camden Yards baseball park, one-third of the Orioles' 3.5 million fans came from the Washington area.

Both Washington, D.C., and Baltimore play their roles as regional centers very well as do, for example, Atlanta, Boston, Minneapolis, San Francisco, and much-maligned New York City. There is one regional role, however, in which these cities cannot succeed—and which may ultimately crush them. They cannot continue as human warehouses for most of their metro areas' poor minorities. However glittering their downtowns, many of their neighborhoods are slowly dying.

The erosion is not so much physical. Many older neighborhoods in Washington, D.C., are physically very attractive—an urban regentrifier's paradise. It is the social chemistry that has gone awry.

I hope that no one who has read to this point still interprets my arguments as being solely a plea for fiscal equity—that suburbs should pay the bill for cities to take care of the problems of the metro area's poor. There is no amount of money that can feasibly be spent to accomplish that. "Bad neighborhoods defeat good programs," I have stated. "Ghettos can only become bigger ghettos."

The severity of the social chaos in many inner-city neighborhoods—unemployment, poverty, dependency, illegitimacy, drugs, crime—is a function of the intense concentration and isolation of the poor. The misery of the whole is much greater than the sum of the individual hardships. Inner cities should not have to assume the role of sole providers for the poor. That must become the responsibility of the whole metro area—city and suburbs, cities without suburbs.

A decade ago I argued these themes at the U.S. Conference of Mayors. I got virtually no support. Suburban mayors did not want to think about central cities. They believed their constituents had said goodbye and good riddance to the city. Central city mayors—more and more, Black or Hispanic—did not want to hear any proposals that might threaten their political comfort levels. After all, Black and Hispanic communities had waited a long time to achieve real power at city hall.

A decade later the need for radical action is much more acute, yet the choruses of "empowerment" continue to swell. I am not unsympathetic. But a vision rises before my eyes. The *Titanic* has just hit the iceberg. The captain turns to his long-time first mate and says, "Here. You take charge. I'm outta here." It is a pretty empty promotion for the first mate. It is also no consolation to the poor people stowed away in steerage who cannot get off the sinking ship.

My metaphor is exaggerated. Being mayor of a major city is no empty honor or responsibility. Cities are still important, and having Black and Hispanic mayors is important for the entire society.

The solution, however, is not to watch from the safety of the *Carpathia* as the great ship goes down. Help get many of the people in steerage into the lifeboats. Keep a crack crew on board to repair the tears in the ship's fabric and recruit more adventuresome, well-heeled passengers to come back on board again. Promote the former first mate to admiral of the fleet.

Throughout this book I have not focused enough on one key element of solving the urban problem: what to do about inner-city public schools? Many middle-class families make decisions about where to live largely based on the quality of local schools. Inner-city neighborhoods can be repeopled with middle-class households without children if neighborhoods are made safer. Re-attracting middle-class households with children to many city neighborhoods requires dramatic improvements in schools. And, of course, the children who are already in inner-city schools most need and deserve better schools.

In no way have I meant to ignore the challenge nor to downgrade the central importance of the quality of local schools in city revival. But the mix of children in the classroom is another of the issues that is no longer discussed in Washington. Most proposals to reform urban education strike me as another version of the nonargument between Big Buckers and Big Bootstrappers over urban policy. Education reform, however, is a topic for another book.

One final observation. Metro government will strike many people as smacking of Big Brother. In many ways the belief that "smaller government is better government" resonates emotionally within me as well.

As Albuquerque grew, more and more residents felt the loss of the small-town atmosphere they had treasured. One of my antidotes to "bigness" was to encourage "smallness." City hall actively promoted the growth of neighborhood associations. From nineteen neighborhood associations when I took office, the neighborhood movement grew to over ninety associations four years later.

Most neighborhood associations are like army reserve units. They have their community picnics in local parks once or twice a year (like two weeks of summer encampment), but they are not mass movements year-round. They are kept alive by a small cadre of professional activists, but they are there to provide a framework for mass mobilization when a crisis occurs.

In city life a neighborhood crisis most often happens when neighbors believe that someone is going to do something to the neighborhood: a developer proposes an apartment building on the edges of a single-family home neighborhood, or the city government plans to put a drug-treatment center in an old mansion, or—the nuclear war of city planning—the state highway department revives old freeway plans right through the area.

Faced with almost any proposed change in the area, neighborhood associations are profoundly conservative. They are typically against any proposal for well-enumerated reasons. Months of meetings and public hearings usually follow. Ultimately, if the proposal is not killed by neighborhood opposition, the final result is a compromise plan that is generally better, on balance, than the original project.

Any forward progress, however, requires a willingness by the planning commission, the city council, and the mayor to push forward for what is in the interests of the larger community. If left strictly to the preferences of the neighborhood association (and the city councillor from that area), *nothing* would ever happen.

What has happened in much of urban America is analogous. In many areas public responsibility and public accountability have become so fragmented that nobody will act for the good of the larger community. In so many metro areas, local government has become little but an agglomeration of large-scale neighborhood associations. No overall planning commission or city council or mayor has a comprehensive vision and the courage to act for all. It is time for governors and state legislators to step into that void.

Note

1. Bill Clinton and Al Gore, *Putting People First: How We Can All Change America* (New York: Times Books, 1992), p. 52.

Appendix

Central Cities and Metro Areas by Elasticity Category

This appendix ranks central cities by their relative elasticity within the different categories outlined in Chapter II for metropolitan areas. Both central cities and metropolitan areas are listed as defined for the 1990 census. The cities are ranked in ascending order of elasticity. In each table the most inelastic city is ranked first in the "zero elasticity" column. The most elastic city will be listed last in the "hyper elasticity" column.

These rankings are often more art than exact science. Cities with sharply different circumstances can sometimes have the same elasticity score. I have generally given the edge to rate of expansion in municipal area rather than initial residential density. Readers should not get caught up in slight differences in elasticity rankings among cities, but focus on where each city falls within the broad categories.

In each table a city that is in all capital letters (for example, OAKLAND, Calif.) is considered to be the primary or historic central city for that metro area. A city in lower case (for example, Berkeley, Calif.) is considered to be a secondary central city. In all instances where two or more central cities are designated in a metro area's title, I have chosen the first named. Thus, MINNE-APOLIS, Minnesota, is the primary central city and St. Paul, Minnesota, is the secondary central city.

An asterisk (*) following a city's name indicates that the city was already considered a central city in the 1950 census.

145 Central Cities over 100,000 Population in 117 Large Metro Areas[a]

Zero Elasticity	Low Elasticity	Medium Elasticity	High Elasticity	Hyper Elasticity
NEW YORK, N.Y.*	HONOLULU, Hawaii*	RICHMOND, Va.*	Pomona, Calif.	San Bernardino, Calif.*
NEWARK, N.J.*	TACOMA, Wash.*	SOUTH BEND, Ind.*	RIVERSIDE, Calif.	SANTA ROSA, Calif.
BOSTON, Mass.*	NEW ORLEANS, La.*	PORTLAND, Oreg.*	FORT LAUDERDALE, Fla.	FORT WORTH, Tex.*
ST. LOUIS, Mo.*	Hampton, Va.	LANSING, Mich.*	Hollywood, Fla.	SAN DIEGO, Calif.*
DETROIT, Mich.*	Stamford, Conn.*	Newport News, Va.	Tempe, Ariz.	CORPUS CHRISTI, Tex.*
WASHINGTON, D.C.*	DAYTON, Ohio*	LEXINGTON, Ky.*	BATON ROUGE, La.*	HOUSTON, Tex.*
PITTSBURGH, Pa.*	ALLENTOWN, Pa.*	ANN ARBOR, Mich.	MEMPHIS, Tenn.*	JACKSON, Miss.*
CLEVELAND, Ohio*	ERIE, Pa.*	SACRAMENTO, Calif.*	LINCOLN, Nebr.*	LITTLE ROCK, Ark.*
SAN FRANCISCO, Calif.*	SEATTLE, Wash.*	Hialeah, Fla.	STOCKTON, Calif.*	VALLEJO, Calif.
PATERSON, N.J.	Long Beach, Calif.	ROCKFORD, Ill.*	SAN ANTONIO, Tex.*	Irving, Tex.
PHILADELPHIA, Pa.*	GRAND RAPIDS, Mich.*	DENVER, Colo.*	COLUMBUS, Ga.*	HUNTSVILLE, Ala.
BUFFALO, N.Y.*	NORFOLK, Va.*	OMAHA, Nebr.*	JACKSONVILLE, Fla.*	LAS VEGAS, Nev.
PROVIDENCE, R.I.*	PEORIA, Ill.*	GARY, Ind.	PHOENIX, Ariz.*	LUBBOCK, Tex.*
BALTIMORE, Md.*	LOS ANGELES, Calif.*	DES MOINES, Iowa*	SHREVEPORT, La.*	RENO, Nev.
HARTFORD, Conn.*	ATLANTA, Ga.*	CHARLOTTE, N.C.*	SALINAS, Calif.	GREENSBORO, N.C.*
MINNEAPOLIS, Minn.*	SAVANNAH, Ga.*	INDIANAPOLIS, Ind.*	BEAUMONT, Tex.*	ORLANDO, Fla.*
ROCHESTER, N.Y.*	FLINT, Mich.*	ANAHEIM, Calif.	FRESNO, Calif.*	MONTGOMERY, Ala.*
	TOLEDO, Ohio*	OXNARD, Calif.	RALEIGH, N.C.*	Arlington, Tex.
	EVANSVILLE, Ind.*	St. Petersburg, Fla.*	DALLAS, Tex.*	TALLAHASSEE, Fla.
	Waterbury, Conn.*	BIRMINGHAM, Ala.*	MODESTO, Calif.	OKLAHOMA CITY, Okla.*
			MOBILE, Ala.*	BAKERSFIELD, Calif.
				TUCSON, Ariz.
				COLORADO SPRINGS, Colo.

SYRACUSE, N.Y.*
JERSEY CITY, N.J.*
CHICAGO, Ill.*
ALBANY, N.Y.*
Berkeley, Calif.
BRIDGEPORT, Conn.*
MILWAUKEE, Wis.*
Elizabeth, N.J.
NEW HAVEN, Conn.*
St. Paul, Minn.*
Lowell, Mass.*
MIAMI, Fla.*
OAKLAND, Calif.*
WORCESTER, Mass.*
SPRINGFIELD, Mass.*
LOUISVILLE, Ky.*
Arlington, Va.
CINCINNATI, Ohio*

COLUMBUS, Ohio*
Pasadena, Calif.
AKRON, Ohio*
Portsmouth, Va.*
FORT WAYNE, Ind.*

NASHVILLE, Tenn.*
WICHITA, Kans.*
Santa Ana, Calif.
MADISON, Wis.*
KANSAS CITY, Mo.*
MACON, Ga.*
KNOXVILLE, Tenn.*
Kansas City, Kans.
TAMPA, Fla.*
TULSA, Okla.*

Durham, N.C.*
Winston Salem, N.C.*
CHATTANOOGA, Tenn.*
ALBUQUERQUE, N. Mex.*
SAN JOSE, Calif.*

AUSTIN, Tex.*
Virginia Beach, Va.
Escondido, Calif.
Mesa, Ariz.
ANCHORAGE, Alaska
Scottsdale, Ariz.

aMetro areas with 200,000 or more residents in 1990.

185 CENTRAL CITIES UNDER 100,000 POPULATION IN 48 LARGE METRO AREAS[a]

Zero Elasticity	Low Elasticity	Medium Elasticity	High Elasticity	Hyper Elasticity
Evanston, Ill.	Springfield, Ohio*	Annapolis, Md.	SANTA BARBARA, Calif.	Marietta, Ga.
Cambridge, Mass.	GALVESTON, Tex.*	North Chicago, Ill.	FORT PIERCE, Fla.	North Little Rock, Ark.*
Camden, N.J.	Leominster, Mass.	COLUMBIA, S.C.*	Kent, Ohio	Jacksonville, Ark.
Norristown Brgh, Pa.	CHARLESTON, S.C.*	Norman, Okla.	SANTA CRUZ, Calif.	Palm Springs, Calif.
Pawtucket, R.I.	Oak Ridge, Tenn.	Attleboro, Mass.	Woodland, Calif.	Boca Raton, Fla.
NEW BRUNSWICK, N.J.	Middleton, Conn.	Northampton, Mass.	ROANOKE, Va.*	Delray Beach, Fla.
Miami Beach, Fla.	Rome, N.Y.*	Westfield, Mass.	Bowling Green, Ohio	Slidell, La.
TRENTON, N.J.*	East Chicago, Ind.	Suffolk, Va.	Ventura, Calif.	Turlock, Calif.
READING, Pa.*	Port Huron, Mich.	New Albany, Ind.	Bristol, Va.	FAYETTEVILLE, N.C.
Lawrence, Mass.*	Burbank, Calif.	Elgin, Ill.	Davis, Calif.	WEST PALM BEACH, Fla.
WILMINGTON, Del.*	White Plains, N.Y.	Mishawaka, Ind.	Midland, Mich.	Chapel Hill, N.C.
Lynn, Mass.	Waltham, Mass.	Belleville, Ill.	Texas City, Tex.	HICKORY, N.C.
Perth Amboy, N.J.	Pontiac, Mich.	LORAIN, Ohio*	Petersburg, Va.	Warner Robins, Ga.
Schenectady, N.Y.*	SARASOTA, Fla.	Lodi, Calif.	Lompoc, Calif.	FORT MYERS, Fla.
POUGHKEEPSIE, N.Y.	AUGUSTA, Ga.*	Alton, Ill.	Napa, Calif.	Leavenworth, Kans.
Woonsocket, R.I.	HAMILTON, Ohio*	Lancaster, Ohio	St. Charles, Mo.	Bossier City, La.
New Britain, Conn.*	Carlisle Brgh, Pa.	PENSACOLA, Fla.	DAVENPORT, Iowa*	DAYTONA BEACH, Fla.
ATLANTIC CITY, N.J.*	Alliance, Ohio	BOULDER, Colo.	Longmont, Colo.	Auburn, Wash.
Hoboken, N.J.	Warren, Ohio	Pekin, Ill.	LAFAYETTE, La.*	VISALIA, Calif.
HARRISBURG, Pa.*	Brockton, Mass.*	Granite City, Ill.	Port Arthur, Tex.*	Temple, Tex.
YORK, Pa.*	Holyoke, Mass.*	Framingham, Mass.	GAINESVILLE, Fla.	
McKeesport, Pa.	Bloomington, Ill.	Haverhill, Mass.	BRADENTON, Fla.	
Easton, Pa.*	Rock Island, Ill.*	Monterey, Calif.		

CANTON, Ohio*
NEW LONDON, Conn.
LANCASTER, Pa.*
Troy, N.Y.*
NIAGARA FALLS, N.Y.
UTICA, N.Y.*
East St. Louis, Ill.
Salem, Mass.
Dearborn, Mich.
Hammond, Ind.
Fall River, Mass.*
Norwalk, Conn.*
KALAMAZOO, Mich.*
Lebanon, Pa.
YOUNGSTOWN, Ohio*
NEW BEDFORD, Mass.*
SAGINAW, Mich.*
Bay City, Mich.*
Kannapolis, N.C.
Milford, Conn.
Norwich, Conn.
Seaside, Calif.

Barberton, Ohio
Moline, Ill.*
East Lansing, Mich.
Bethlehem, Pa.*
JOLIET, Ill.
Meriden, Conn.
Fitchburg, Mass.
Bristol, Conn.*
Bloomington, Minn.

Chicago Heights, Ill.
Spartanburg, S.C.
Newark, Ohio
Gloucester, Mass.
GREENVILLE, S.C.*
Elkhart, Ind.
Massillon, Ohio
WAUKEGAN, Ill.
Petaluma, Calif.
Bessemer, Ala.
Danbury, Conn.
Fairfield, Calif.

West Memphis, Ark.
Council Bluffs, Iowa
Clearwater, Fla.
Rock Hill, S.C.
Elyria, Ohio*
Baytown (Part), Tex.
Frederick, Md.
Everett, Wash.
Tulare, Calif.
High Point, N.C.*
JOHNSON CITY, Tenn.
Kingsport, Tenn.
Bristol, Tenn.
Winter Haven, Fla.
Gastonia, N.C.
Santa Maria, Calif.
Palo Alto, Calif.

Pompano Beach, Fla.
Livermore, Calif.
KILEEN, Tex.
Porterville, Calif.
Murfreesboro, Tenn.
LAKELAND, Fla.
Shawnee, Okla.
MELBOURNE, Fla.
Denton, Tex.
Titusville, Fla.
AURORA, Ill.
Roseville, Calif.
Olathe, Kans.
Palm Bay, Fla.

aMetro areas with 200,000 or more residents in 1990.

TABLE A-3

144 CENTRAL CITIES UNDER 100,000 POPULATION IN 122 SMALL METRO AREAS[a]

Zero Elasticity	Low Elasticity	Medium Elasticity	High Elasticity	Hyper Elasticity
ELMIRA, N.Y.	BENTON HRBR, Mich.	LAWRENCE, Kans.	ATHENS, Ga.	TUSCALOOSA, Ala.
SHARON, Pa.	LEWISTON, Maine*	DUBUQUE, Iowa	MEDFORD, Oreg.	BATTLE CREEK, Mich.
JAMESTOWN, N.Y.	Auburn, Maine	FARGO, N. Dak.	FLORENCE, Ala.	JACKSONVILLE, N.C.
STATE COLLEGE, Pa.	Millville, N.J.	GREAT FALLS, Mont.	ANNISTON, Ala.	MIDLAND, Tex.
GLEN FALLS, N.Y.	BILLINGS, Mont.	TERRE HAUTE, Ind.*	ST. CLOUD, Minn.	OLYMPIA, Wash.
Dunkirk, N.Y.	BELLINGHAM, Wash.	VINELAND, N.J.	PINE BLUFF, Ark.	GREEN BAY, Wis.*
KENOSHA, Wis.*	PITTSFIELD, Mass.*	JACKSON, Tenn.	JOPLIN, Mo.	VICTORIA, Tex.
LIMA, Ohio*	RACINE, Wis.*	SIOUX CITY, Iowa*	CHEYENNE, Wyo.	Denison, Tex.
CHAMPAIGN, Ill.	SHEBOYGAN, Wis.	BANGOR, Maine	GREELEY, Colo.	TYLER, Tex.
OWENSBORO, Ky.	Bridgeton, N.J.	West Lafayette, Ind.	FLORENCE, S.C.	MERCED, Calif.
JACKSON, Mich.*	HAGERSTOWN, Md.	Rantoul Village, Ill.	FORT SMITH, Ark.-Okla.	Texarkana, Ark.
BURLINGTON, Vt.	KOKOMO, Ind.	SPRINGFIELD, Ill.*	TEXARKANA, Tex.	FORT COLLINS, Colo.
DECATUR, Ill.*	PUEBLO, Colo.*	ST. JOSEPH, Mo.*	LAKE CHARLES, La.	Loveland, Colo.
BLOOMINGTON, Ind.	GRAND FORKS, N. Dak.	CASPER, Wyo.	Gulfport, Miss.	DECATUR, Ala.
ANDERSON, S.C.	LAFAYETTE, Ind.	BURLINGTON, N.C.	ANDERSON, Ind.	ENID, Okla.
MUSKEGON, Mich.	Urbana, Ill.	ALEXANDRIA, La.	WICHITA FALLS, Tex.*	COLUMBIA, Mo.
	Thibodaux, La.	LA CROSSE, Wis.	SAN ANGELO, Tex.*	WACO, Tex.*
	MUNCIE, Ind.*	MONROE, La.	IOWA CITY, Iowa	

KANKAKEE, Ill.
BILOXI, Miss.
WILMINGTON, N.C.
BLOOMINGTON, Ill.
Beloit, Wis.
BREMERTON, Wash.
MANSFIELD, Ohio
HOUMA, La.
FRT WLTN BCH, Fla.
PANAMA CITY, Fla.
YAKIMA, Wash.
CHRLTTSVILLE, Va.
TOPEKA, Kans.*
GADSDEN, Ala.*

ROCHESTER, Minn.
EAU CLAIRE, Wis.
NAPLES, Fla.
WAUSAU, Wis.
SANTA FE, N. Mex.
ABILENE, Tex.
DANVILLE, Va.
ELKHART, Ind.
YUBA CITY, Calif.
DOTHAN, Ala.
Moorhead, Minn.

WATERLOO, Iowa*
ODESSA, Tex.
CEDAR RAPIDS, Iowa*
Goshen, Ind.
BISMARCK, N. Dak.
SIOUX FALLS, S. Dak.*
PASCAGOULA, Miss.
JANESVILLE, Wis.
ASHEVILLE, N.C.*

BRYAN, Tex.
Kennewick, Wash.
Hopkinsville, Ky.
AMARILLO, Tex.*
YUMA, Ariz.
LYNCHBURG, Va.
Normal Town, Ill.
LAWTON, Okla.
RAPID CITY, S. Dak.
CHICO, Calif.
LONGVIEW, Tex.
RICHLAND, Wash.
LAS CRUCES, N. Mex.
Cedar Falls, Iowa
Pasco, Wash.
ALBANY, Ga.
Springdale, Ark.
FAYETTEVILLE, Ark.
SHERMAN, Tex.
OCALA, Fla.
CLARKSVILLE, Tenn.
College Station, Tex.
REDDING, Calif.

aMetro areas with fewer than 200,000 residents.

TABLE A-4
FOUR SPECIAL CATEGORIES

Zero Elasticity	Low Elasticity	Medium Elasticity	High Elasticity	Hyper Elasticity
Mexican Border Towns in 4 Metro Areas				
Harlingen, Tex.			LAREDO, Tex.* Edinburg, Tex. Pharr, Tex. BROWNSVILLE, Tex. Mission, Tex.	McALLEN, Tex. EL PASO, Tex.*
		Declining Mining Regions		
ALTOONA, Pa.* Wilkes-Barre, Pa.* JOHNSTOWN, Pa.* WILLIAMSPORT, Pa. CUMBERLAND, Md. HUNTINGTON, W. Va.* Hazelton, Pa.* STEUBENVILLE, Ohio* SCRANTON, Pa.* Weirton, W. Va. WHEELING, W. Va.*	CHARLESTON, W. Va.* PARKERSBURG, W. Va.	Superior, Wis.* Ashland, Ky.* DULUTH, Minn.* Marietta, Ohio		

White-America Cities in 13 Metro Areas

BINGHAMTON, N.Y.*

Nashua, N.H.
Rochester, N.H.
MANCHESTER, N.H.*
Oshkosh, Wis.
PORTLAND, Maine*
PORTSMOUTH, N.H.

VANCOUVER, Wash.
Dover, N.H.
APPLETON, Wis.
SPOKANE, Wash.*
Neenah, Wis.

Ogden, Utah
Orem, Utah
Springfield, Oreg.
SALT LAKE CITY, Utah*
SPRINGFIELD, Mo.*
SALEM, Oreg.

PROVO, Utah
BOISE, Idaho
EUGENE, Oreg.

City-Less Metro Areas

NASSAU-SUFFOLK, N.Y.
MONMOUTH-OCEAN, N.J.
ORANGE COUNTY, N.Y.
BRAZORIA, Tex.
BEAVER VALLEY, Pa.

Note from the Author

The research summarized in *Cities without Suburbs* is built upon a self-compiled data base that, as hard copy, would equal the length of the book itself. To economize in length and cost, the publisher and I decided not to include the data base as an appendix to this book.

However, I am eager to assist public officials, citizens, planning professionals, academic researchers, and students grappling with the complex problems of metropolitan areas.

Therefore, I am publishing separately the data by which I calculated the elasticity scores for all central cities as the *Cities without Suburbs Data Supplement*. For all 522 central cities the supplement will provide population density (1950 and 1990), percentage relative to national density average (1950), population density ranking by decile (1950), city area (1950 and 1990), city area expansion ranking by decile (1950–1990), elasticity score, and capture/contribute ratio.

The data supplement may be purchased for $15.00 per copy from David Rusk, 4100 Cathedral Avenue, NW, #610, Washington, D.C. 20016; (202) 364-2455.

Sources

All data not otherwise indicated are taken from publications of the Bureau of the Census of the U.S. Department of Commerce. These publications cover the decennial censuses from 1950 to 1990.

The sources for municipal bond ratings are *Moody's State and Local Government Data Book (1991)* and direct inquiries to city finance departments.

The calculations of residential segregation rates are drawn from Roderick J. Harrison and Daniel H. Weinberg, ''Racial and Ethnic Segregation in 1990,'' U.S. Bureau of the Census, Washington, D.C., April 1992.

Similar calculations on school segregation have been made by Maris Mikelsons and Jeff Mosley of the Urban Institute and myself. Our data come from tapes prepared by the National Center for Education Statistics of the U.S. Department of Education.

Per capita income data are drawn from the 1990 census, the Census Bureau's *State and Metropolitan Area Data Book 1991* and earlier editions (including the *City and County Data Book*). Based on census data, I have calculated suburban per capita incomes in 1989 myself.

All information on metro area employment trends, including manufacturing employment, comes from *Regional Projections to 2040: Volume 2 Metropolitan Statistical Areas*, published by the U. S. Commerce Department's Bureau of Economic Analysis (October 1990).

The analysis of state laws regarding city-county consolidation, municipal formation, and annexation powers is adapted from Melvin B. Hill, Jr., et al., *State Laws Governing Local Government and Administration*, Institute of Government, University of Georgia (1971). The information has been ably updated by my research assistant, Daniel Greene.

Information on changes in city minority population from 1980 to 1990 has been helpfully provided by Professor William H. Frey of the University of Michigan's Population Studies Center.

Information on regional civic organizations has been drawn from recent copies of the *National Civic Review*, published six times a year by the National Civic League. I have also quoted or paraphrased extensively from the NCL's proposal, "Regional Civic Governance: Emerging Organizational Structures and Strategies" (August 1991).

Finally, I am indebted to the inspiration provided by Professor Hank V. Savitch (University of Louisville), in particular "Ties That Bind: Central Cities, Suburbs, and the New Metropolitan Region" (unpublished paper). I also have referred to Hank V. Savitch, "The Regional City and Public Partnerships," in *In the National Interest: The 1990 Urban Summit*, The Twentieth Century Fund Press, New York, 1992. The material quoted in the Afterword is taken from personal correspondence from Dr. Savitch commenting on my manuscript.

Index

ACIR (U.S. Advisory Commission on Intergovernmental Relations), 113–14, 125–26

age, city's: elasticity ratings and, 66; as factor in expansion, 23, 25–28; and racial segregation, 35

Albuquerque (New Mexico): economic integration in, 116; total community package in, 70

Anchorage (Alaska), successful annexation by, 10

annexation: of Chesterfield County by Richmond (Virginia), 26–27; example of, described, 53; and state laws, 20–22, 98–100, 124; and urban expansion, 9–10, 16–24, 20–21, 26–27, 88; see also consolidation

Bay Vision 2020 (San Francisco Bay region), 118

Blacks: and ghetto expansion, 78–79; see also minorities; racial segregation

bond ratings, municipal: and elasticity ratings, 74–76; of paired metro areas, 43–45

"capture or contribute," cities and suburban growth, 20, 21

central cities: elasticity ratings of, 131–41; of paired metro areas, 14–15

Chesterfield (Virginia), annexation of, by Richmond, 26–27

Chicago Housing Authority (CHA), 114–15

cities without suburbs: criteria for, 78–79, 82; examples of, 82–83; table of, 80–81

citizen initiatives, for creating metro government, 116–19, 125–26

city-suburb income gaps, see income ratio

Confluence St. Louis, 117–18

consolidation: of Indianapolis and Marion County, 93; of Nashville and Davidson County, 94; rarity of, 96; and state laws, 97–98, 124; and urban expansion, 16, 25; as way to create metro government, 92, 94–95; see also annexation

county government, 91–92, 95, 124

data base, used for book, 143

Davidson County (Tennessee), consolidation of, and Nashville, 94

deindustrialization: effect of, on urban areas, 38–40; and elasticity ratings, 70–73

"dissimilarity" index, 30, 36

economic integration: in Albuquerque, 116; in elastic cities, 31–33

economic segregation: and elasticity ratings, 63–69; as focus of urban policy, 121–30; in paired metro areas, 31–33; policies for diminishing, 123

economy: interdependence of city, and suburban, 74–75; and paired metro areas, 38–40; see also elasticity ratings; urban expansion

elastic cities: and annexation, 9–10, 16, 20–21; composite profile of, 47–48; economic integration in,

143

The Woodrow Wilson International Center for Scholars

The Center is the "living memorial' of the United States of America to the nation's twenty-eighth president, Woodrow Wilson. The U.S. Congress established the Woodrow Wilson Center in 1968 as an international institute for advanced study, "symbolizing and strengthening the fruitful relationship between the world of learning and the world of public affairs." The Center opened in 1970 under its own presidentially appointed board of directors.

Woodrow Wilson Center Special Studies

The work of the Center's Fellows, Guest Scholars, and staff and presentations and discussions at the Center's conferences, seminars, and colloquia often deserve timely circulation as contributions to public understanding of issues of national and international importance. The Woodrow Wilson Center Special Studies series is intended to make such materials available by the Woodrow Wilson Center Press to interested scholars, practioners, and other readers. In all its activities, the Woodrow Wilson Center is a nonprofit, nonpartisan organization, supported financially by annual appropriations from the U.S. Congress, and by the contributions of foundations, corporations, and individuals. Conclusions or opinions expressed in Center publications and programs are those of the authors and speakers and do not necessarily reflect the views of the Center's staff, Fellows, Trustees, advisory groups, or any individuals or organizations that provide financial support to the Center.